Incomes and Productivity in North America

Papers from the 1997 Seminar

Commission for Labor Cooperation
North American Agreement on Labor Cooperation

Co-published by Bernan Press and the
Commission for Labor Cooperation

Secretariat of the Commission for Labor Cooperation
One Dallas Centre
350 North St. Paul
Suite 2424
Dallas, Texas 75201-4240 USA

www.naalc.org
214.754.1100
fax 214.754.1199

Distributed by
Bernan Associates
4611-F Assembly Drive
Lanham, MD 20706-4391 USA

www.bernan.com
800.274.4447
fax 800.865.3450

This collection of papers was compiled by Alfredo Hernández,
International Cooperative Activities Coordinator at the Secretariat.
Each author is solely responsible for the contents of his or her paper.

Cover design: Alejandro Magallanes/La Máquina del Tiempo

ISBN (English) 0-89059-087-7
ISBN (French) 0-89059-088-5
ISBN (Spanish) 0-89059-089-3

Contents

List of Figures

Chapter 6. Labor Market Developments, Trade,
and Trade Agreements

Chapter 8. The Challenge of Workplace Innovation in Canada

List of Tables

Foreword

The North American Seminar on Incomes and Productivity has been organized under the auspices of the Commission for Labor Cooperation, which is a new international institution created by the North American Agreement for Labor Cooperation (NAALC).

This new Commission is headed by a Council of Ministers, which comprises the Minister of Labour of Canada, the Secretary of Labor and Social Welfare of México, and the Secretary of Labor of the United States. The Council of Ministers is supported by an international Secretariat located in Dallas.

The Commission for Labor Cooperation is an example of what a leading Canadian legal scholar, Harry Arthurs, calls "new institutions for the new economy." That we have a "new economy" is not news anymore, nor that it is characterized by rapid technological change, which is based on information technology, globalization of production and markets, transformation of the nature of work, and so forth. Later in this seminar, we will hear the phrase "the new techno-economic paradigm."

But it is worth noting, as perhaps there is less attention paid to this fact, that this new economy is calling forth new institutions to cope with its new dimensions. Some of these are new international institutions; we might think of the World Trade Organization (WTO) or, closer to home, of the Chapter 19 or Chapter 20 dispute resolution mechanisms of the North American Free Trade Agreement (NAFTA), which are very significant innovations themselves in the institutionalization of international trade relations.

Moreover, not all of these new institutions are limited to strictly commercial or "economic" subject matter. In the case of NAFTA, we have seen the creation of new institutions for labor and for environmental matters. The reason is these fields are recognized as having an integral connection with the emerging international economy.

The NAFTA labor agreement is probably best known so far for its objectives on labor law enforcement—and this response is understandable. The labor agreement creates an unprecedented innovation in international labor affairs by establishing an international discipline related to the enforcement of domestic labor laws. This system provides a new form of international support to the rule of law in the labor area among trading partners, and it is the world's first such agreement on labor standards linked to a trade agreement.

But a less well recognized fact is that the scope of the NAFTA labor agreement goes far beyond its provisions regarding labor law enforcement. Among the seven primary "Objectives" of the agreement are to improve working conditions and living standards in each party's territory, and to encourage cooperation that promotes innovation and rising levels of productivity and quality.

Similarly, the agreement includes the parties' resolution "to promote high-skill, high-productivity economic development in North America."

In support of these broad economic objectives, the Commission provides an institutional framework through which all three countries can work in a spirit of economic cooperation and development. The NAALC explicitly recognizes that the mutual prosperity of the three countries can be improved by such cooperation.

It is probably axiomatic that as international competition increases in the new economy, international cooperation must also increase. The objective is to provide the necessary international infrastructure and framework—just as domestic laws and institutions do within nations—

to ensure that the vast energy of competition is channeled most productively while its risks are minimized.

This seminar, in fact, was the first activity under the auspices of the Commission for Labor Cooperation (since its creation in 1994) to be directed to economic questions. Other activities have focused on labor laws and their administration, in such areas as labor relations, safety and health, and child labor. But with this seminar, the Commission sponsored its first public activity regarding the economy of the labor markets in North America as the Commission focuses on the central questions of productivity and incomes and on how those two critical labor market factors interrelate.

We hope to provide a forum for dialogue between labor, business, and academic sectors across the three NAFTA countries, with government in a listening mode. We also hope this dialogue will improve our common understanding of questions of central importance within a context that recognizes the common situation that all in North America share.

John S. McKennirey
Executive Director
Secretariat of the Commission
    for Labor Cooperation
March 1997

Introduction

The linkage between incomes and productivity has always been under debate. Economic globalization has added new ingredients to the debate. Bearing in mind this situation, the Council of Ministers of the Commission for Labor Cooperation of the North American Agreement for Labor Cooperation (NAALC) asked the Secretariat to undertake an ongoing forum. This forum will conduct a high-level and constructive debate among labor, business, and academia representatives from the North American Free Trade Agreement (NAFTA) countries while the governments listen.

To meet this petition, the Secretariat set up a Steering Committee comprising John McKennirey, Chairman and Executive Director, Secretariat of the Commission for Labor Cooperation; Professor Gonzalo Hernández, Instituto Technológico Autónomo de México (ITAM), Mexico; Professor Anthony Giles, Laval University, Canada; Professor Leonard Bierman, Texas A&M University, United States; Dr. Leoncio Lara, Director, Secretariat; and Alfredo Hernandez, Secretariat and Seminar Coordinator. The committee was in charge of the first North

American Seminar on Incomes and Productivity, and it provided every panelist a list of topics that could be addressed for this first event, thereby allowing panelists plenty of liberty to define their own approach. Broad outlines were as follows:

1. Macroeconomics Perspective: Wages, Productivity, and Competitiveness in the North American Labor Markets

- What have been the trends in productivity growth and incomes, and how do these trends relate to competitiveness and North American economic interaction?
- Is there a gap developing between labor output and wages? How is the distribution of income evolving in the three labor markets, and what is its significance?
- How could trade, especially within North America, affect these issues? How do the labor markets interact?
- What are the positive signs, what are the risks, and what are the long-term policy questions for the future of incomes and productivity in North America?

2. Microeconomics Perspective: The Changing Employment Relationship in the Open Economy

- If there is declining job security, what is emerging as the alternative source of economic security for workers in the new, open economy of North America?
- What are the implications for the employment relationship of the imperative for constantly improving productivity? Is there a new "deal" between employers and employees?
- What new structures are emerging in the employment relationship—worker capital participation, labor laws, labor-management relations, corporate governance—and how do these structures relate to income and productivity?

The seminar was the first-ever event linking academic and private sectors in the three NAFTA countries with each other and with the Commission. The seminar put together a high-level group of experts and participants who are from Canada, Mexico, and the United States and who are deeply involved in the analysis and practices of incomes and productivity in the region. The agenda of the seminar was designed for promoting constructive dialogue among the panelists and with the audience. The agenda gave an equal opportunity for presenting various points of view on each issue.

The academic speakers were Professor Alan B. Krueger, Princeton University; Professor Daniel Trefler, University of Toronto/University of Chicago; Dr. José Alberro, Consultoría de Diseño de Estrategias; Professor Edward Wolff, New York University; Dr. Gordon Betcherman, Ekos Research Associates/Canadian Policy Research Network; Dr. Ray Marshall, University of Texas at Austin; and Professor Norma Samaniego, Universidad Iberoamericana/Sante Fe Consultores. The business respondents were Chuck Nielson, Vice President of Human Resources of Texas Instruments; Carlos Gutiérrez, President, Cámara Nacional de la Industria de la Tranformación; Adolfo Tena, Confederación Patronal de la República Mexicana; and Sam Boutzlouvis, Business Council on National Issues–Canada. The labor respondents were Gilberto Muñoz-Mosqueda, Secretario General del Sindicato de Trabajadores de la Industria Química, Petroquímica, Carboquímica, Similares y Conexos de la República Mexicana; Gérald Larose, President, Confédération des syndicats nationaux–Quebec; Steven M. Beckman, United Auto Workers/AFL–CIO; and Andrew Jackson, Canadian Labour Congress.

The moderators of the two public sessions were business members of the National Advisory Committees on the NAALC from Mexico and the United States: Jorge de Regil from Confederación Nacional de Cámaras Industriales and Carroll Bostic from Eastman Kodak Company, respectively. In Appendix B of this book, you will find a complete list of all attendees.

This volume collects the papers presented in the "1997 North American Seminar on Incomes and Productivity" held on February 28, 1997, in Dallas, Texas, and sponsored by the Secretariat of the Commission for Labor Cooperation in collaboration with the ITAM, North American Policy Studies Program; Laval University–Quebec, Department of Industrial Relations; and Texas A&M University–University of Texas at Austin, Center for the Study of Western Hemispheric Trade.

In the seminar's first panel session, "Wages, Productivity, and Competitiveness in the North American Labor Markets," three well-known academic economist professors (Edward N. Wolff, Daniel Trefler, and

José Alberro) presented original research papers on this topic, using their own country as a reference point. The comments presented in writing by labor representatives Andrew Jackson and Steven Beckman are also included in this volume.

A luncheon keynote address followed the first session. Professor Alan B. Krueger gave an exposition on "Labor Market Developments, Trade, and Trade Agreements."

For the second panel session, three well-known researchers (Ray Marshall, Gordon Betcherman, and Norma Samaniego) presented original research papers on "Changing Labor Relations in an Open Economy." Written comments by Carlos Gutiérrez, Gilberto Muñoz, and Gérald Larose are also presented in this volume.

Alfredo Hernández
Seminar Coordinator
April 1997

CHAPTER 1

Per Capita Income and Relative Productivity Performance in Canada, Mexico, and the United States, 1950–1994

Edward N. Wolff
New York University

This article provides a scorecard on the performance of the three North American Free Trade Agreement (NAFTA) countries (Canada, Mexico, and the United States) during 1950–1994. It begins by presenting aggregate trends in productivity, per capita income, and related measures of economic performance over the post–World War II period for the three economies. It also analyzes some of the factors responsible for the relative trends in these three countries.

Trends in Per Capita Income and Productivity

I will begin with Summers and Heston's data (forthcoming) from their new Penn World Tables Mark 5.6, which provide information for 1950–1992 on real per capita gross domestic product (GDP) for 150 countries, including the three NAFTA countries. Summers and Heston express these data in 1985 "international dollars," arrived at by using purchasing power parity (PPP) exchange rates (now accepted as a method far superior to that of using currency exchange rates) to convert each country's raw GDP figures. This standardized set of statistics, which Summers and Heston refer to as real GDP (RGDP), makes it possible to compare the economic performance of countries at four levels of development: industrialized, middle income, centrally planned, and less developed. The data are also updated to 1994 on the basis of the World Bank Socioeconomic Time-series Access and Retrieval System (STARS) database.

As shown in table 1.1 and figure 1.1, Mexico had the highest growth in per capita income of the three countries, followed by Canada and then the United States. Table 1.1 uses two different measures of per capita income. The first is the conventional Laspeyres Index GDP per capita (RGDPL). For Mexico, the annual average growth rate in RGDP was 2.4 percent from 1950 to 1994; for Canada, it was 2.2 percent; and for the United States, 1.7 percent. However, while the growth in per capita income was rather continuous for the United States and Canada, it was much more uneven for Mexico. Indeed, between 1950 and 1981, RGDPL grew at an annual rate of 3.51 percent. Between 1981 and 1987, RGDPL actually fell in absolute terms, from $6,467 to $5,262, or by *3.44 percent per year.* Since bottoming out in 1987, GDP per capita has been growing rather steadily, and in 1994 it reached $6,243, for an annual growth rate over this period of 2.44 percent, close to Mexico's post–World War II average.

Another way to look at the same trend is in relation to the U.S. level of RGDPL (see figure 1.2 and the addendum to table 1.1). In 1995, Canada's GDP per capita (RGDPL) stood at 73 percent of the United States level of $8,648. However, Canada gained steadily on the United States, and by 1989, Canada had reached $17,519, or 97 percent of the corresponding U.S. level. Since that time, Canada's RGDPL has fallen not only relative to the U.S. level, but also in absolute terms. Thus in 1993, its RGDPL was only $16,548, or 90 percent of the corresponding U.S. level. In the case of Mexico, RGDP was only 25 percent of the U.S. level in 1950. However, by 1981, it had reached 42 percent of the corresponding U.S. level, but then it slipped to a low of 30 percent in 1988. By 1994, it was back to 33 percent of the U.S. level—the same relative position it enjoyed in 1977.

Table 1.1. Real GDP Per Capita in Canada, Mexico, and the United States, 1950–1994[a]

	Year								Annual Growth Rate
	1950	1960	1970	1980	1990	1992	1993	1994	
RGDPL: Real GDP per Capita (Laspeyres index)									1950–1994
Canada	6,324	7,240	10,122	14,133	17,179	16,371	16,548	—	2.24b
Mexico	2,179	2,825	3,985	6,051	5,825	6,250	6,139	6,243	2.39
United States	8,648	9,908	12,969	15,311	18,073	17,986	18,406	18,953	1.78
RGDPCH: Real GDP per Capita (chain index)									1950–1992
Canada	6,380	7,258	10,124	14,133	17,173	16,362	—	—	2.24
Mexico	2,198	2,836	3,987	6,054	5,827	6,253	—	—	2.49
United States	8,772	9,895	12,963	15,295	18,054	17,945	—	—	1.70
RGDPEA: Real GDP per Equivalent Adult									1950–1990
Canada	7,493	8,720	11,925	15,926	19,220	—	—	—	2.35
Mexico	2,801	3,675	5,199	7,798	7,243	—	—	—	2.38
United States	10,136	11,713	15,097	17,234	20,295	—	—	—	1.74
RGDPW: Real GDP per Worker									1950–1990
Canada	16,113	19,484	24,906	28,725	34,380	—	—	—	1.89
Mexico	6,824	9,517	14,086	18,890	17,012	—	—	—	2.28
United States	20,496	24,433	30,468	31,698	36,771	—	—	—	1.46

(continued on next page)

Table 1.1. Real GDP Per Capita in Canada, Mexico, and the United States, 1950–1994[a] (continued)

	Year							
	1950	1960	1970	1980	1990	1992	1993	1994
Addendum: Percentage of U.S. Level								
RGDPL: Real GDP per Capital (Laspeyres index)								
Canada	73	73	78	92	95	91	90	—
Mexico	25	29	31	40	32	35	33	33
United States	100	100	100	100	100	100	100	100
RGDPCH: Real GDP per Capital (chain index)								
Canada	73	73	78	92	95	91	—	—
Mexico	25	29	31	40	32	35	—	—
United States	100	100	100	100	100	100	—	—
RGDPEA: Real GDP per Equivalent Adult								
Canada	74	74	79	92	95	—	—	—
Mexico	28	31	34	45	36	—	—	—
United States	100	100	100	100	100	—	—	—
RGDPW: Real GDP per Worker								
Canada	79	80	82	91	93	—	—	—
Mexico	33	39	46	60	46	—	—	—
United States	100	100	100	100	100	—	—	—

[a] All figures are in 1985 international prices. Sources are 1950–1992, Penn World Tables (PWT) 5.6; 1993–1994, World Bank STARS database.

[b] 1950–1993.

Figure 1.1. RGDPL—Real GDP per Capita

(1985 international prices [Laspeyres], 1950–1994)

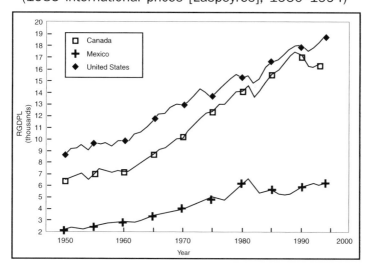

Figure 1.2. RGDPL—Real GDP per Capita

(as a ratio to U.S. level, 1950–1994)

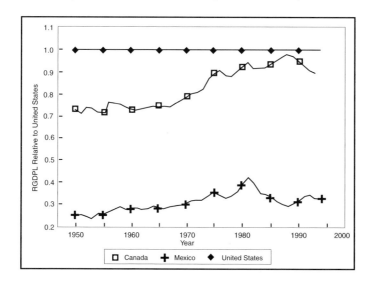

Results from the three other indices are similar. The first of these is real GDP capita based on a chain index (RGDPCH). The results are almost identical to those based on RGDPL. The second is real GDP per equivalent adult (RGDPEA). This index is more of a welfare measure in which children are converted into adult equivalents by using their relative amount of consumption. For this index as well, the time trends are quite similar, although this index goes only to 1990. However, Mexico does better in terms of this index because Mexico has a higher proportion of children in its population. Its level of RGDPEA relative to the U.S. level rose from 28 percent in 1950 to 45 percent in 1980, but it fell to 36 percent by 1990.

The last of these indices is real GDP per worker (RGDPW). This index is more of a labor productivity index than a per capita welfare measure. According to this index, Mexico began in 1950 at 33 percent of the U.S. level (compared with 25 percent based on GDP per capita) and by 1980 had reached *60 percent* of the U.S. level (compared with 40 percent for per capita income). By 1990, it was back to only 46 percent of the U.S. level.

Investment, Trade, and Education

A state of economic backwardness does not in itself guarantee that a nation will go on to catch up with, or even move toward, the world's titans. Many other factors must be present in the underdeveloped but aspiring economy; they include strong investment, as well as an educated and well-trained work force, a significant amount of research and development activity, a developed information sector, a suitable product mix, a set of developed trading relations with advanced countries, a program of foreign investment by multinational corporations, a receptive political structure, and a low population growth. In this section, I will report on some variables that affect the convergence process.

The principal requirements for convergence, or catch-up, have been identified by researchers, including myself, in a large number of earlier studies, so I will simply summarize the cross-country analysis (Baumol, Blackman, and Wolff 1989; Barro 1991). The first requirement, or variable, for catch-up is investment. It is generally agreed that two primary ingredients are present in the growth of labor productivity: (1) technological innovation and (2) the accumulation of capital through saving. Most studies find that innovation and the international transfer of the products of innovation have played the major role in converging productivity levels of a number of relatively successful industrialized economies. But many studies find that, in addition, substantial capital accumulation is required to put the inventions into practice and to ensure their widespread employment.

A second important variable in the catch-up process is education. The statistical evidence supports the hypothesis that the level of education provided by an economy to its inhabitants is one of the major influences determining whether per capita income in a country is growing rapidly enough to narrow the gap with per capita income in the more advanced economies.

A third important variable in the catch-up process is the extent of openness of an economy, or the degree to which a country is involved in trade with other countries. Countries with more open economies have been found to have higher rates of productivity catch-up than those that close their borders to trade. Interestingly, openness to imports from other countries appears to be a stronger influence than the degree to which a country exports its products abroad. This result is consistent with the "advantages of backwardness" argument, since imports from advanced countries provide a direct source of information on new technology to the backward country.

A fourth crucial influence or variable, particularly for the developing world, appears to be the rate of population growth. Too-rapid population growth can swamp any gains from the advantages of backwardness. Any gains in productivity from introducing new technology may be offset and, as a result, will not increase per capita income.

Table 1.2 shows trends in these key variables for the three NAFTA countries. With regard to the investment rate (panel A of table 1.2 and figure 1.3), Canada and the United States have clearly been ahead of Mexico in the post–World War II period. The average investment rate for Canada in 1950–1994 was 24.1 percent; for the United States, 21.4 percent; and for Mexico, only 15.8 percent. Canada's investment rate

Table 1.2. Comparative Statistics on Investment, Trade, Population Growth, and Educational Enrollment Rates, Period Averages, 1950–1994[a]

	1950–1959	1960–1969	1970–1979	1980–1989	1990–1994	1950–1994
A. Real Investment as a Percentage of GDP (1985 international prices)—PWT 5.6						
Canada	24.4	23.0	23.1	25.2	26.4[b]	24.1[b]
Mexico	13.7	15.6	18.0	16.1	15.3[b]	15.8[b]
United States	21.9	22.0	21.5	21.0	19.4[b]	21.4[b]
B. Merchandise Exports as a Percentage of GDP (1987 U.S.$)—World Bank						
Canada		15.5	19.9	22.8	27.0[c]	20.3[c]
Mexico		11.4	6.8	15.4	24.2[c]	12.7[c]
United States		3.9	5.5	6.0	7.9	5.5
C. Merchandise Imports as a Percentage of GDP (1987 U.S.$)—World Bank						
Canada		17.2	23.0	21.4	25.8[c]	21.2[c]
Mexico		11.7	11.0	14.2	29.1[c]	14.3[c]
United States		4.5	6.9	8.3	10.2	7.1

(continued on next page)

Table 1.2. Comparative Statistics on Investment, Trade, Population Growth, and Educational Enrollment Rates, Period Averages, 1950–1994[a] (continued)

	1950–1959	1960–1969	1970–1979	1980–1989	1990–1994	1950–1994
D. Exports of Goods and Non-Factor Services as a Percentage of GDP (1987 U.S.$)—World Bank						
Canada		16.2	20.5	25.3	30.8[c]	21.9[c]
Mexico		11.4	10.6	16.8	20.4	14.0
United States		4.8	6.7	8.0	11.3[c]	7.1[c]
E. Imports of Goods and Non-Factor Services as a Percentage of GDP (1987 U.S.$)—World Bank						
Canada		14.1	18.6	24.0	32.0[c]	20.4[c]
Mexico		15.4	16.3	16.7	30.0	18.1
United States		5.4	7.8	9.9	12.8[c]	8.3[c]
F. Population Growth (percentage annual growth rate) 1950–1959—PWT 5.6; 1960–1994—World Bank						
Canada	2.67	1.76	1.46	1.20	1.17	1.69
Mexico	3.17	3.13	2.87	2.32	2.08	2.79
United States	1.72	1.29	1.05	0.93	1.04	1.21

(continued on next page)

17

Table 1.2. Comparative Statistics on Investment, Trade, Population Growth, and Educational Enrollment Rates, Period Averages, 1950–1994[a] (continued)

	1950–1959	1960–1969	1970–1979	1980–1989	1990–1994	1950–1994
G. Primary School Gross Enrollment Rate —World Bank[d]						
Canada		1.05	1.00	1.05	1.07[b]	1.04[b]
Mexico		0.92	1.13	1.18	1.14[b]	1.08[b]
United States		1.00	0.99	1.01	1.04[b]	1.00[b]
H. Secondary School Gross Enrollment Rate —World Bank[e]						
Canada		0.56	0.85	1.01	1.04[b]	0.83[b]
Mexico		0.17	0.36	0.53	0.55[b]	0.37[b]
United States		0.63	0.89	0.94	0.90[b]	0.83[b]
I. Gross Enrollment Rate in Higher Education —World Bank[f]						
Canada		0.26		0.58		0.42[g]
Mexico		0.04		0.15	0.15	0.10[b]
United States		0.40	0.56	0.60	0.90	0.54[b]

[a] Sources are Penn World Tables (PWT) 5.6 and World Bank STARS database.
[b] 1992.
[c] 1993.
[d] Primary school enrollment as a proportion of primary school age group, averaged between 1965 and 1983.
[e] Secondary school enrollment as a proportion of secondary school age group, averaged between 1965 and 1983.
[f] Enrollment in higher (university) education as a proportion of university age group, averaged between 1965 and 1983.
[g] 1989.

Figure 1.3. Investment as a Percentage of GDP, 1950–1992

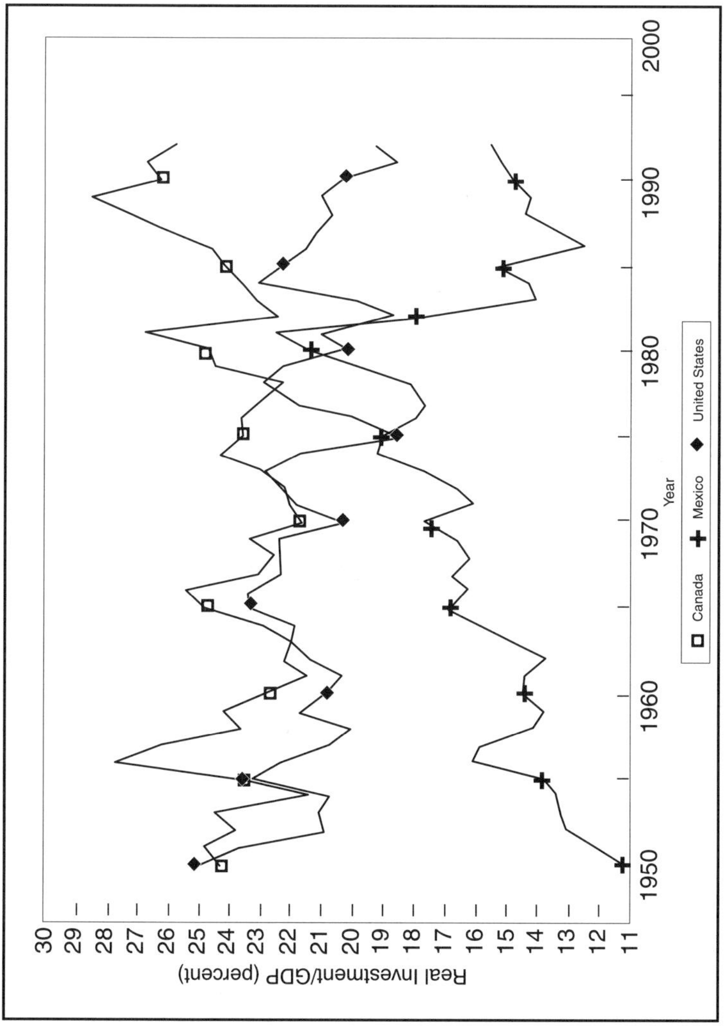

has been rising gradually during this period, from 24.4 percent in the 1950s to 26.4 percent in 1950–1994. The Mexican investment rate showed a sharp rise from 13.7 percent in the 1950s to 18.0 percent in the 1970s, but the rate has since fallen off to 15.3 percent in the early 1990s. The U.S. investment rate has been virtually flat from the 1950s to the 1980s, averaging between 21 and 22 percent, and it was down somewhat in the early 1990s, at 19.4 percent.

Of the three NAFTA countries, Canada has been the most open, followed by Mexico and the United States. As shown in panel B of table 1.2, Canada's merchandise export share (of GDP) averaged 20.3 percent over 1960–1994, while Mexico's merchandise export share averaged only 5.5 percent. However, all three countries have shown increasing trade openness over the post–World War II period. Canada's export share (of GDP) increased from an average of 15.5 percent in the 1960s to 27.0 percent in the early 1990s. At the same time, Mexico's export share increased from 11.4 percent in the 1960s to 24.2 percent in the early 1990s, and the U.S. export share went from 3.9 percent to 7.9 percent.

The results are similar for merchandise imports as a share of GDP (see panel C of table 1.2). Canada was the most open economy in this dimension as well, followed by Mexico and then the United States. Moreover, all three countries showed rising import shares during 1960–1994. However, interestingly, there was a sharp decline in Mexico's import openness in the mid-1980s, reflecting the heavy protectionism of this era, but a strong recovery occurred by 1987 (see figure 1.5). Indeed, Mexico overtook Canada in terms of openness in this dimension by the early 1990s.

The results are again similar in exports of goods and nonfactor services as a percentage of GDP and in imports of goods and nonfactor services as a percentage of GDP (see panels D and E of table 1.2, plus figures 1.4 and 1.5). Canada led all three countries by these two indices as well, and all three countries showed increases over 1960–1994. Mexico again overtook Canada in terms of import openness by 1992.

As shown in panel F of table 1.2, population growth has been considerably higher in Mexico than in the other NAFTA countries during post–World War II—2.8 percent per year in Mexico compared

Figure 1.4. Total Exports as a Percentage of GDP, 1960–1994

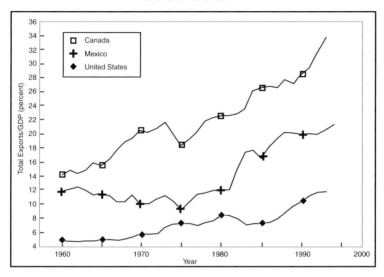

Figure 1.5. Total Imports as a Percentage of GDP, 1960–1994

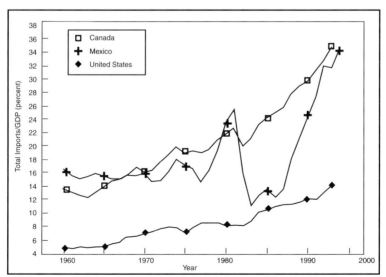

with 1.69 percent per year in Canada and 1.21 percent per year in the United States. However, all three countries, particularly Mexico, showed sharp declines in population growth in that period: Mexico from 3.2 percent per year in the 1950s to 2.1 percent per year in the early 1990s; Canada from 2.7 percent to 1.2 percent in the same period; and the United States from 1.7 percent in the early 1950s to 1.0 percent in the 1970s, then remaining almost unchanged through the early 1990s.

As shown in the last three panels of table 1.2, all three countries have shown very high enrollment rates in primary school during the entire postwar period—100 percent or better in almost all cases (since the figures are gross enrollment rates, they can exceed 100 percent). All three countries have also shown sharp improvements in their enrollment rates for secondary schools: Canada from 56 percent in the 1950s to 104 percent in the early 1990s, Mexico from 17 percent to 55 percent, and the United States from 63 percent to 90 percent. Interestingly, Canada had a higher enrollment rate in secondary schools than the United States by the early 1990s. Indeed, the U.S. enrollment rate in secondary schools fell somewhat from the 1980s to the early 1990s—probably reflecting the large influx of Hispanic immigrants over this period.

However, the United States appears to have maintained its lead in college enrollment rates. Those rates rose from 40 percent in the 1950s to 74 percent in the early 1990s. In comparison, Canada's higher education enrollment rate increased from 26 percent in the 1950s to 58 percent in the 1980s, and Mexico's rose from 4 percent in the 1950s to only 15 percent by the early 1990s.

Conclusion

We are now in a position to qualitatively evaluate some of the evidence regarding the relative performance of the three NAFTA economies over the post–World War II period. With regard to Canada and the United States, the former's higher overall growth rate in both GDP per capita and labor productivity largely reflects the so-called "catch-up phenomenon"—the finding that countries whose level of productivity is behind that of the leading countries of the world will gain more in terms of knowledge and technology than the leading countries will gain from the laggards (see Baumol, Blackman, and Wolff 1989, chap. 5). The fact that Canada started the postwar period at 73 percent of the U.S. level in terms of RGDPL by itself explains most of Canada's higher productivity growth. In addition, the fact that Canada had a higher investment rate than the United States, as well as greater import and export openness, also helps explain its higher growth rate.

On the negative side of the ledger are the findings of a higher rate of population growth in Canada than in the United States, as well as lower enrollment rates in higher education in Canada than in the United States. However, these variable by themselves do not appear to explain the strong fall-off in per capita income growth experienced by Canada after 1989, both in absolute terms and relative to the United States. Some Canadian economists have argued that the very restrictive monetary policy of the Canadian central bank during the early 1990s may be responsible for this setback.

With regard to Mexico and the United States, the catch-up effect also explains a large part of Mexico's higher growth in both per capita income and labor productivity over the whole postwar period. Also in Mexico's favor are its greater degree of trade openness and the fact that both export and import intensity rose more rapidly in Mexico than in the United States. In addition, though population growth over this entire period was considerably higher in Mexico than in the United States, it declined more in Mexico than in the United States between the 1950s and early 1990s. Conversely, the fact that the investment rate was considerably higher in the United States than in Mexico and the fact that enrollment rates in both secondary and higher education (particularly the latter) were also higher in the United States than Mexico retarded per capita income growth in Mexico relative to the United States.

The other peculiar finding is that Mexico made considerable gains on the United States in both per capita income and labor productivity from 1950 to 1981, fell in both absolute terms and relative to the United States from 1981 to 1987, and has since made modest relative gains on the United States. The evidence I have presented does suggest some reasons for this time trend. First, Mexico's investment rate peaked in the 1970s, declined in the 1980s, and declined even further in the early 1990s. Second, whereas Mexico made considerable progress in both its secondary and higher education enrollment rates between the 1960s and 1980s, it failed to make further gains in the early 1990s. Third, a very sharp decline in Mexico's import openness occurred exactly in the mid-1980s, which limited Mexico's acquisition of new technology from abroad.

Bibliography

Barro, Robert J. "Economic Growth in a Cross Section of Countries." *Quarterly Journal of Economics* 106, no. 2 (May 1991): 407–43.

Baumol, William J.; Sue Anne Batey Blackman; and Edward N. Wolff. *Productivity and American Leadership: The Long View.* Cambridge, Mass.: MIT Press, 1989.

Summers, Robert, and Alan Heston. "Penn World Trade (Mark 5.6), 1950–1992." Forthcoming.

CHAPTER 2

No Pain, No Gain: Lessons from the Canada–U.S. Free Trade Agreement

Daniel Trefler
Institute for Policy Analysis, University of Toronto
Harris Public Policy School, University of Chicago

Economists are fixated on the benefits of international trade agreements. Free trade raises productivity, wages, and consumer welfare by forcing countries to specialize in the narrower range of goods for which they have a cost advantage. But lurking behind this tale of industrial restructuring are laid-off workers; workers must leave high-cost, import-competing industries in search of new jobs. To the dismal scientist, it is taken for granted that without industrial restructuring and its handmaiden of worker layoffs there can be no benefits from free trade. To an unemployment-weary Canadian workforce seeking job security, nothing could be more cruel than this message of "no pain, no gain."

I am grateful to Alberto Isgut for his able research assistance. The financial support provided by the Social Security and Humanities Research Council of Canada is gratefully acknowledged.

This paper paints a balanced picture of the costs and benefits of the Canada–U.S. Free Trade Agreement (CAFTA) in January 1989.* Attention is restricted to the tradables sector, which includes manufacturing, natural resources, and agriculture. I will document that CAFTA brought on the destruction of 138,000 jobs, or 6 percent of the tradables workforce. Paradoxically, this job destruction was set against a large increase in production. CAFTA raised value added by $3.5 billion, or 3 percent, since the start of the agreement. Value added is the sum of labor and capital costs. This jobless recovery—job losses and output expansion—is explained by rising productivity. For industries previously protected by tariffs, CAFTA raised productivity by a remarkable 2.5 percent per year. This gain is from industrial restructuring and is a vindication of the economists' message.

The pain, of course, is lost jobs. And rising productivity was not translated into more money in the pockets of workers who kept their jobs; where productivity growth was most rapid, wage growth was most sluggish. To top things off, CAFTA contributed to rising wage inequality.

On balance, Canada gained $50,000 per lost job for a job that pays $26,000 per worker. Restated, society can afford a 2-year severance package for each lost job. This "side payment" still leaves society with the benefits of lower consumer prices. Conversely, this calculus ignores wage stagnation and exacerbated income inequality. The CAFTA scorecard: B minus. What follows is a more detailed analysis.

Q. Why did the tradables sector (manufacturing, natural resources, and agriculture) lose one in every four jobs right after implementation of CAFTA?

A. • After a prolonged, 7-year expansion, a recession was due.
   • The Bank of Canada fought against inflation, raised interest rates, and strengthened the dollar.
   • Relative to that of the United States, Canadian productivity had been eroding for years.
   • The Canada–United States Free Trade Agreement took effect.

Lost Jobs Peaked in 1993

Jobs are the number one issue in the Canadian economy and so serve as a benchmark for evaluating the performance of CAFTA. Figure 2.1 plots the lost jobs in the tradables sector since 1988. The lost jobs peaked in 1993, with about 400,000 jobs lost. This figure amounts to 23 percent of the jobs in the tradables sector. The figure has since fallen to 290,000, which still represents 15 percent of the workforce.

Figure 2.1. Lost Jobs in the Tradables Sector since CAFTA
(January 1989)

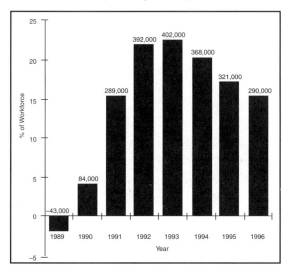

It has been common in the Canadian press to attribute most of these job losses to CAFTA. Unfortunately, the economy has been subjected to a number of other changes in the interim. The most important of these changes was the recession that was exacerbated by the Bank of Canada's battle against inflation (Fortin 1996; Gaston and Trefler 1997).

To disentangle the effects of CAFTA from other events, I adopted the treatment-control framework familiar from the medical literature (Card and Krueger 1994). The control group consists of those industries that had very low or nonexistent tariffs before 1989. It is dominated by the natural resource and automotive sectors. Against this are two types of patients. The first is the high-tariff group of industries. In 1988, the year preceding implementation of CAFTA, these industries had tariff rates of between 8 percent and 23 percent. The group is primarily composed of the textile, clothing, and leather products industries. These are industries that one expects to be hard hit by CAFTA because they cannot compete on labor costs with southern U.S. states.[1] The second is the low-tariff group with pre-CAFTA rates of between 3 percent and 6 percent. This diverse group of industries includes food products, steel, and pharmaceuticals. The effect of CAFTA here is less clear. Some firms will recognize their comparative disadvantage and will either cease operations or relocate in the South. Other firms will recognize the tremendous advantage of access to the U.S. market and will respond with aggressive capital improvements to existing plants, a trimming of product lines to lengthen production runs, new marketing campaigns, and other innovations.

The treatment-control framework starts by randomly assigning subjects (industries) to a control, or placebo, group and a treatment group. The different responses of the two groups are then attributed to the treatment. In a similar vein, the different experiences of the high-tariff and low-tariff groups relative to the control group will be attributed to CAFTA.

All of this requires one to believe that the groups are really similar, except for exposure to CAFTA tariff reductions. Yet the fact that the groups have different tariffs is itself evidence of differences. Table 2.1 offers additional qualifications. The groups were constructed so that each employs about 700,000 workers, or one-third of the tradables sector's labor force. The groups differ most in terms of productivity as measured by value added per worker. Productivity and wages differ significantly as between the high-tariff and control groups: the control group is twice as productive and pays one-third more.[2]

Table 2.1. Tradables-Sector Characteristics[a]

	Tariff Rate (percent)	Employment	Value Added (millions)	Productivity (VA per worker)	Weekly Earnings
High-Tariff Group	10.0	743,000	$22,000	$30,000	$427
Low-Tariff Group	5.6	708,000	44,000	62,000	554
Control Group	0.7	724,000	49,000	68,000	569
Total, Tradables	4.4	2,176,000	115,000	53,000	516

[a] The tradables sector includes manufacturing, natural resources, and agriculture.

Q. How many of the lost jobs are attributable to CAFTA?

A. • In 1996, 138,000 of the 290,000 lost jobs were caused by CAFTA.

Figure 2.2 plots lost jobs since 1988 for the high-tariff and control groups. For example, the control group shrank 7 percent between 1988 and 1996, whereas the high-tariff group shrank 17 percent. The high-tariff group contracted about twice as much as the control group, indicating large CAFTA-induced job losses. The bottom panel of figure 2.2 plots the difference between the high-tariff and the control group employment contractions. For example, in 1996 the difference was about 10 percent (17%–7%). One can translate this figure into jobs lost by multiplying by the 1988 employment level in the high-tariff group, which gives an estimate of 74,000 lost jobs in 1996.

Figure 2.3 plots corresponding numbers for the low-tariff industries. Trade theory is unclear about the prediction here, though I would have predicted modest job gains. However, even the low-tariff group experienced significant employment reductions relative to the control group. By 1996, the low-tariff group had contracted by 16 percent, or 9 percent more than the control group. This figure translates into 64,000 lost jobs as of 1996. Summing the losses of the two groups yields 138,000 lost jobs.

Figure 2.2A. Employment Losses Since 1988: High-Tariff Industries

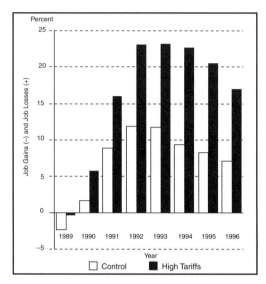

Figure 2.2B. CAFTA-Induced Job Losses Since 1988 in High-Tariff Industries

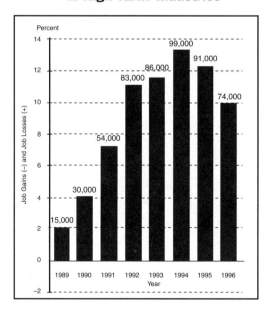

Figure 2.3A. Employment Losses Since 1988:
Low-Tariff Industries

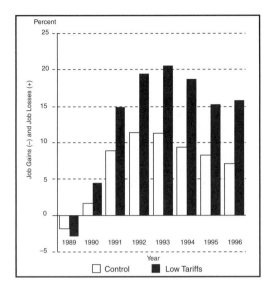

Figure 2.3B. CAFTA-Induced Job Losses Since 1988:
Low-Tariff Industries

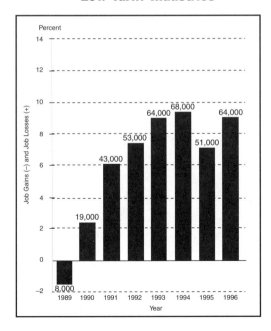

Q. Why were so many jobs lost? Did CAFTA allow U.S. firms to compete more successfully?

A. • For high-tariff industries, output contracted in response to competitive pressures from U.S. firms. CAFTA reduced 1996 output by $2 billion.

• A reduction was not so for low-tariff industries. CAFTA increased 1996 output by a much larger $5 billion.

• The cumulative 1988–1996 effect was a $12 billion rise in Canadian value added.

Figures 2.4 and 2.5 display the value-added growth since 1988. As expected, value added stagnated in the high-tariff group. Relative to the control group during 1988–1996, value added contracted by 8 percent, or about $2 billion. (Note that $2 billion is 8 percent of 1988 value added in the low-tariff group. Also, all data are in 1986 constant dollars.) The cumulative output loss since 1989 was $9 billion. The results for the low-tariff industries are surprising. Relative to the control group during 1988–1996, output grew by 12 percent, or $5 billion. The cumulative effect was a $21 billion increase in output. Summing over the high- and low-tariff industries, 1996 output rose by $3.5 billion and cumulative output rose by $12 billion.

Q. Why were so many jobs lost in the low-tariff industries even though output expanded? Is CAFTA implicated in this jobless recovery?

A. • CAFTA brought about remarkable productivity growth of 5 percent per year. More output was produced with fewer workers.

• Had productivity not grown so fast, 74,000 jobs would have been created in the low-tariff group and only 50,000 jobs lost in the high-tariff group.

• Had productivity not grown so fast, 24,000 new jobs would have been created instead of 138,000 jobs destroyed.

In the low-tariff group, output grew by 2.5 percent per year. At the same time, employment shrank by 2.1 percent per year (see table 2.2).

Figure 2.4A. Value-Added Growth Since 1988: High-Tariff Industries

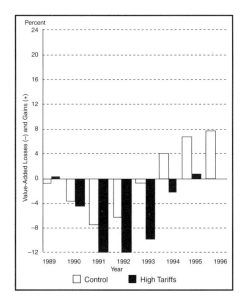

Figure 2.4B. CAFTA-Induced Value-Added Growth Since 1988: High-Tariff Industries

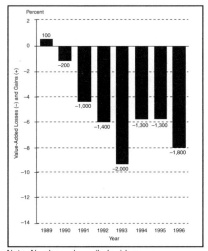

Note: Numbers above (below) bars are millions of 1986 dollars.

Figure 2.5A. Value-Added Growth Since 1988: Low-Tariff Industries

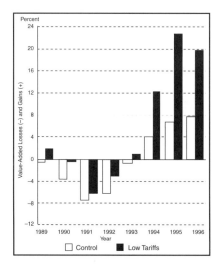

Figure 2.5B. CAFTA-Induced Value-Added Growth Since 1988: Low-Tariff Industries

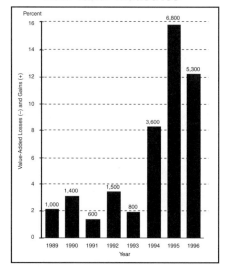

Note: Numbers above bars are millions of 1986 dollars.

While this type of jobless recovery permeated the economy, it was most pronounced in the low-tariff group. Jobless recovery is intimately related to productivity since productivity is often measured as value added per worker:

(1)   PROD = VA/WORKER

where PROD is productivity, VA is value added, and WORKER is employment. It follows that productivity grows by the difference between output and employment growth,[3]

(2)   %PROD = %VA − %WORKER

where "%" means percentage of change.

Table 2.2. Average Annual Growth Rates, 1988–1996[a]

	Employment Growth (percent)	Value Added Growth (percent)	Productivity Growth (percent)	CAFTA Job Losses Net of Productivity Growth
Control	−0.9	1.0	2.0	—
High	−2.1	0.0	2.5	50,000 Jobs Lost
Low	−2.0	2.5	5.3	74,000 Jobs Gained

[a] The growth rate between 1988 and 1996 divided by the number of years (8). See endnote 3 for an explanation of why equation (2) does not hold exactly.

Table 2.2 shows productivity growth. It was dramatically highest for the low-tariff group. *Table 2 provides a vindication of comparative advantage theory. Removing tariffs dramatically improved productivity in the sector that stood to benefit most from access to the larger U.S. market.*

This growth in productivity leads one to wonder what job losses would have been like had they been driven by output changes rather than by rising productivity. While lost jobs by any other name are still lost jobs to those afflicted, the fact is that rising productivity is the core of rising national living standards and so needs to be figured into the credit side of the CAFTA balance sheet. One way of doing this is to ask what employment would have been had productivity in the low- and high-tariff groups grown at the same rate as productivity in the control group. Roughly, employment can be projected by rewriting equation 2 as[4]

(3) $\%WORKER^*_{HIGH} = \%VA_{HIGH} - \%PROD_{CONTROL}$

and

(4) $\%WORKER^*_{LOW} = \%VA_{LOW} - \%PROD_{CONTROL}.$

For the low-tariff group, the result is that we now have 74,000 jobs gained instead of 64,000 jobs destroyed. For the high-tariff group, we have 50,000 jobs destroyed instead of 74,000 jobs destroyed. Summing over the two groups gives 24,000 jobs created rather than the actual 138,000 jobs destroyed. Clearly, most of the job destruction is associated with CAFTA-induced productivity gains.

Q. Does this change in the creation and loss of jobs mean rising productivity in each industry or a shift of output to industries with high productivity?

A. • Most of the change reflects rising productivity in each industry.

• CAFTA had little effect on the productivity of high-tariff industries, but raised productivity in the low-tariff industries by an enormous 4 percent annually.

Why Did Productivity Rise?

The trouble with aggregate productivity numbers is that they are very difficult to interpret. Did productivity rise because of a shift in the composition of output from low-productivity to high-productivity industries? Or did productivity rise in each industry? Two good examples of the latter appear in the data. Consider the manufacturing of electrical products (excluding household appliances and household receivers), which is the largest industry in the low-tariff group. Over 1988–1996, that industry experienced a 100 percent increase in output and a 25 percent decline in employment. This figure translates into a 166 percent increase in productivity. This increase is clearly an example of how CAFTA enabled the industry to thrive. Furniture and fixtures is a medium-sized industry in the high-tariff group. Under CAFTA, that industry was expected to disappear and indeed showed every sign of doing so in the early years of the agreement. However, the industry has made something of a comeback with Palliser Furniture of Winnipeg leading the way. Over the 1988–1996 period, industry value added held its own in the face of intense U.S. competition, employment fell by 24 percent, and productivity rose by 33 percent.

We can return to the treatment-control framework to analyze the effects of CAFTA on productivity. I calculated productivity growth in each industry and then calculated the group average using 1988 employment and value-added weights.[5] Figure 2.6 plots average annual productivity growth for each of the three groups. High-tariff industries experienced productivity growth only 0.4 percent higher than control-group industries; CAFTA had little effect. In contrast, average productivity growth in low-tariff industries outstripped growth in control-group industries by 4 percent. This growth is a remarkable testament to the benefits of trade agreements, benefits that play center stage in economic theory.

Q. Has rising productivity been met with rising earnings or wages?

A. • No. Earnings growth (for all workers) was the same in all groups despite rapid productivity growth in the low-tariff group.
    • No. Wages (for workers paid by the hour) declined in all groups despite rising productivity. Further, wages declined most where productivity rose fastest.
    • No. Similar conclusions hold within the low-tariff group.
    • Inequality of rising earnings was most pronounced in the low- and high-tariff industries.

One would hope that rising productivity would be met by rising wages. This has not been the case either across groups or within groups. Table 2.3 ranks groups by average annual productivity growth in the CAFTA period. Despite large differences in productivity growth across the three groups, earnings growth has been the same. For workers paid by the hour, faster productivity growth has been met by faster wage *declines*. Thus, there is no link between productivity and wage growth.

Figure 2.6. Average Annual Productivity Growth, 1988–1996

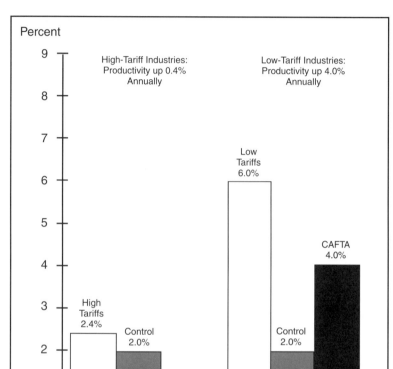

Table 2.3. Average Annual Productivity and Wage Growth, 1988–1996

	Productivity Growth (percent) (1)	Earnings Growth: All Workers (percent) (2)	Wage Growth: Workers Paid by the Hour (percent) (3)	Rising Income Inequality (2) – (3)
Control	2.0	0.5	−0.1	0.6
High	2.4	0.6	−0.6	1.2
Low	6.0	0.5	−1.2	1.8

Within-group results are slightly different. For the control group, we get the expected result that each 1 percent rise in productivity is accompanied by a 0.7 percent rise in earnings. However, for the low-tariff group, we find that each 1 percent rise in productivity is accompanied by a 0.5 percent decline in earnings.

Table 2.3 also provides information on rising income inequality. Salaried workers tend to earn more than workers paid by the hour (Berman, Bound, and Griliches 1994). Thus, all workers (salaried plus hourly) tend to earn more than those paid by the hour. (Variation in hours worked turns out not to be important here.) From table 2.3, earnings have been rising and wages have been falling. Restated, high-paid salaried workers have experienced rising income while low-paid workers have experienced falling incomes. This is evidence of the rising income inequality that has been documented by others. What is remarkable is that rising income inequality has been most pronounced in both the high-tariff and the low-tariff industries, especially the latter. Thus, *CAFTA exacerbated income inequality.*

Q. What is the CAFTA scorecard?
A. • B Minus.
  • It generated enough surplus to cover a 2-year severance package for displaced workers.
  • Consumers benefited from lower prices.
  • Falling wages, rising income inequality, and rising workplace insecurity are all effects of CAFTA.

The effects of CAFTA were remarkably in accord with the theory of comparative advantage. Firms with high tariffs were hit hard both in terms of employment and output. Nevertheless, the firms best positioned to enter the U.S. market thrived. Unfortunately, their productivity growth was so enhanced that jobs were actually lost even in this sector. In addition, the agreement slowed wage growth, worsened income inequality, and raised job insecurity.

It is impossible to quantify all these effects without much more work. However, consider the following: Value added rose by $12 billion, of which approximately two-thirds, or $8 billion, is left after capital expenses. At least 160,000 jobs were lost (the figure for the 1994 trough). This change leaves a $50,000 surplus per job for a job that on average pays $26,000 per year. That figure is enough to cover 2 years of severance pay. While not generous, it is not skimpy either. And the calculus ignores consumer benefits from lower prices. This is a reasonable, but not a stellar, return from policy. I give it a B minus.

Endnotes

[1]Note that U.S. and Canadian tariffs are highly correlated. Industries with high tariffs in one country have high tariffs in the other country.

[2]Other possible differences between the groups are differential responses to business cycles and differential secular movements associated with "deindustrialization." Gaston and Trefler (1997) show this is not a serious issue. To the extent that ignoring these differences results in misleading conclusions, ignoring them biases slightly upward the effect attributed to CAFTA.

[3]More precisely, the formula is

$$\frac{\Pi_{96i} - \Pi_{88i}}{\Pi_{88i}} = \frac{Y_{96i} - Y_{88i}}{Y_{88i}} - \frac{L_{96i} - L_{88i}}{L_{96i}}$$

$$- \frac{Y_{96i} - Y_{88i}}{Y_{88i}} \times \frac{L_{96i} - L_{88i}}{L_{96i}}$$

where:

Π = productivity,

Y = value added,

L = employment, and

i = control, low or high (the group). In table 2.2, employment growth is measured as

$(L_{96i} - L_{88i})/L_{96I}$

Note that the denominator is

L_{96I} rather than L_{88i}.

In table 2.2, employment growth and value-added growth are the first and second terms on the right-hand side, respectively.

[4]More precisely, the equation in endnote 3 can be rewritten as

$L_{96i} = L_{88i} (Y_{96i}/Y_{88i}) / (\Pi_{96i} / \Pi_{88i})$.

Define $L^*_{96LOW} = L_{88LOW} \times (Y_{96LOW}/Y_{88LOW})/(\Pi_{96CONTROL}/\Pi_{88CONTROL})$

where

$\Pi_{96CONTROL}/\Pi_{88CONTROL} = 1.02 \times 8.$

From the control group's productivity growth per year comes 1.02 (2.0%) times the number of years (8). The analysis of the job gains and losses from CAFTA proceeds as before but with L^*_{96LOW} replacing L_{96LOW}. The procedure for the high-tariff group is analogous.

[5]The weights used were 1988 group shares of employment and value added. Using the notation of previous endnotes, define

$\omega_{L,HIGH} = L_{88j}/\Sigma_{j\in HIGH} L_{88j}$ and $\omega_{Y,HIGH} = Y_{88j}/\Sigma_{j\in HIGH} Y_{88j}.$

The weights used for the high-tariff calculations were $(\omega_{L,HIGH} + \omega_{Y,HIGH})/2.$

Bibliography

Berman, Eli; John Bound; and Zvi Griliches. "Changes in the Demand for Skilled Labor Within U.S. Manufacturing Industries: Evidence from the Annual Survey of Manufacturing." *Quarterly Journal of Economics*. (March 1994).

Card, David, and Alan B. Krueger. "Minimum Wages and Employment: A Case Study of the Fast-Food Industry in New Jersey and Pennsylvania." *American Economics Review*. (September 1994).

Fortin, Pierre. "Presidential Address: The Great Canadian Slump." *Canadian Journal of Economics*. (November 1996).

Gaston, Noel, and Daniel Trefler. "The Labour Market Consequences of the Canada–U.S. Free Trade Agreement." *Canadian Journal of Economics*. (February 1997).

CHAPTER 3

Productivity, Trade Liberalization, and Productive Restructuring: The Unequal Performance of the Mexican Economy During 1970–1996

José Luis Alberro-Semerena
Diseño de Estrategias

Over the past 25 years, Mexico has gone through several cycles of boom and bust:

1. The closed-economy, "shared development" model ended up in an 80 percent devaluation in late 1976.

2. The oil boom resulted in the Mexican debt crisis of 1982.

3. After the economy grew at an average annual rate of more than 4 percent during 4 years (1989–1992), there was a financial run several times larger than the 1982 episode that required a $48.8 billion multilateral assistance package. GDP decreased 6.2 percent during 1995, and the ensuing "tequila effect" affected several Latin American stock markets.

The analysis of the structural weaknesses that have led to this macroeconomic instability has rarely considered the behavior of the real sector of the economy. This article analyzes the behavior of productivity during that period and the effect that the trade liberalization

I am grateful to Dolores Nieto and Mario Cuellar for all their research assistance.

process initiated in 1987 had on productive restructuring. It argues that opening the Mexican economy had a decisive impact on Mexico's competitiveness and that the remarkable growth of exports during the past decade reflects such growth. It questions the depth of that restructuring and worries about developing an enclave of *maquiladoras*[1] (in-bond industries located in national territory that establish a contract to process or assemble components and machinery temporarily imported and to re-export them thereafter; by 1988 the *maquiladoras* were allowed to sell a portion of their goods on the domestic market) with weak links to the rest of the economy.

In the next section, I will analyze the behavior of productivity during 1970–1987 and will conclude that its dismal performance fueled criticism against the closed-economy model that had dominated the post–World War II intellectual consensus in Latin America. In the third section, I will argue that while the trade liberalization strategy introduced a decade ago has increased productivity, real earnings seem to reflect macroeconomic factors rather than sectoral conditions. In the fourth section, I will review some evidence of the impact of foreign trade on productivity changes, and in the last section, I will look at the productive restructuring that has occurred during the past few years in the manufacturing sector.

The Behavior of Productivity 1970–1987[2]

During 1970–1987, Total Factor Productivity (TFP) for the economy as a whole barely grew (table 3.1). During the "shared development period" (1970–1976), TFP decreased at an annual rate of 1 percent, and during the López Portillo presidential term, which included the oil boom, TFP did grow, but at a pace of only 1 percent. It stagnated during the De la Madrid Sexenio (1983–1987) part of the last decade.

The only hopeful sign during that last period was the productivity growth in the manufacturing sector, which reached 4.65 percent a year. The growth was led by the basic metal industry, wood, and printing sectors. It should also be noted that the standard deviation of those

Table 3.1. Total Productivity, 1980 Prices
(Average Annual Percentage Growth)

Sectors	1970–1976	1977–1982	1983–1987
2. Mining	–3.66%	–2.14%	–0.91%
3. Manufacturing industry	0.89	0.61	4.65
3.1 Food, beverages, and tobacco	3.41	0.13	4.87
3.2 Textiles, clothing, leather	–1.79	0.72	–8.08
3.3 Wood and wood products	–2.28	–2.11	10.25
3.4 Printing	2.17	1.76	6.02
3.5 Chemical, petroleum derivates, plastics	1.19	3.95	4.72
3.6 Nonmetallic minerals, except oil products	–1.49	0.46	6.63
3.7 Basic metal industries	1.35	–0.97	9.74
3.8 Machinery and equipment	3.20	–1.00	3.51
3.9 Others	–5.14	–5.81	3.46
4. Construction	–1.04	–0.52	1.34
5. Electricity, water, gas	1.13	–0.46	0.22
6. Retailing, restaurants, hotels	–0.88	5.99	–0.78
7. Transportation, communications	–1.05	–1.24	–0.58
8. Financial services	–2.40	2.68	0.35
9. Government services	–0.99	–1.25	–2.14
Total	–0.96	1.06	–0.02
Standard Deviation Across Sectors	3.08	3.51	4.23
Standard Deviation in the Manufacturing Sector	3.62	3.72	4.99

Sources: INEGI, Banco de México, Diseño de Estrategias, S.C.

rates of change increased during the period, signaling a growing divergence not merely among productive sectors, but even within manufacturing.

This stagnant overall performance is composed of offsetting behaviors of the productivities of labor and capital as shown in tables 3.2 and 3.3.

- The average annual rates of growth of labor productivity were positive but decreasing, as was their divergence.
- The average annual rates of growth of capital productivity were negative, and their divergence was high and increasing, particularly after 1977.

Table 3.2. Labor Productivity, 1980 Prices
(Average Annual Percentage Growth)

Sectors	1970–1976	1977–1982	1983–1987
2. Mining	–0.99%	0.12%	0.82%
3. Manufacturing industry	2.67	1.73	1.72
3.1 Food, beverages, and tobacco	2.00	1.38	0.18
3.2 Textiles, clothing, leather	1.09	0.83	–1.15
3.3 Wood and wood products	2.65	0.91	1.77
3.4 Printing	3.74	3.09	1.40
3.5 Chemical, petroleum derivates, plastics	4.89	2.95	1.80
3.6 Nonmetallic minerals, except oil products	4.24	1.83	0.35
3.7 Basic metal industries	2.15	0.46	7.64
3.8 Machinery and equipment	2.87	1.94	3.41
3.9 Others	–3.88	–1.74	0.69
4. Construction	–0.24	–4.25	–1.85
5. Electricity, water, gas	4.09	–0.91	1.58
6. Retailing, restaurants, hotels	4.27	3.37	–1.32
7. Transportation, communications	2.94	–2.18	0.18
8. Financial services	1.03	–1.34	1.93
9. Government services	0.37	0.26	–0.01
Total	2.12	0.53	0.44
Standard Deviation Across Sectors	2.92	3.10	1.80
Standard Deviation in the Manufacturing Sector	2.63	3.01	2.90

Sources: INEGI, Banco de México, Diseño de Estrategias, S.C.

Table 3.3. Productivity of Capital, 1980 Prices
(Average Annual Percentage Growth)

Sectors	1970–1976	1977–1982	1983–1987
2. Mining	–5.23%	–3.16%	–1.59%
3. Manufacturing industry	0.02	0.15	5.84
3.1 Food, beverages, and tobacco	3.82	–0.24	6.49
3.2 Textiles, clothing, leather	3.81	0.65	–11.18
3.3 Wood and wood products	–4.76	–3.28	14.04
3.4 Printing	1.42	1.22	7.88
3.5 Chemical, petroleum derivates, plastics	–0.72	4.44	6.25
3.6 Nonmetallic minerals, except oil products	–3.77	0.04	8.82
3.7 Basic metal industries	0.70	–1.64	10.70
3.8 Machinery and equipment	3.41	–2.52	3.55
3.9 Others	–5.64	–7.00	4.23
4. Construction	–2.04	6.05	10.40
5. Electricity, water, gas	–3.63	0.17	–1.60
6. Retailing, restaurants, hotels	–1.90	6.50	–0.68
7. Transportation, communications	–3.73	–0.74	–0.97
8. Financial services	–2.98	3.40	0.05
9. Government services	–2.91	–2.97	–4.25
Total	–2.39	1.28	–0.19
Standard Deviation Across Sectors	8.22	5.42	5.95
Standard Deviation in the Manufacturing Sector	5.30	4.61	6.68

Sources: INEGI, Banco de México, Diseño de Estrategias, S.C.

We should note that during the whole period, the manufacturing sector had a consistently better performance. Labor productivity grew at close to 2 percent a year during those years. While capital productivity did poorly between 1970 and 1982, it grew at 5.8 percent between 1982 and 1987, led as before by the basic metal industry, wood, and printing sectors.

Several figures at the end of this chapter (figures 3.18–3.23) will show the three types of productivity indexes for each sector, as well as for each segment of the manufacturing industry, using 1980 prices. By 1987, only manufacturing, along with retailing, restaurants, and hotels, had TFPs more than 10 percent above their 1970 level and had labor productivity indexes more than 30 percent above their 1970 level. In turn, the productivity of capital in the three sectors dominated by governmental intervention (electricity, water, and gas; transportation and communications; and government services) had declined between 20 percent and 30 percent.

This dismal productivity performance capped the rate of growth of GDP, exacerbating the macroeconomic imbalances that led to recurrent crises and making the need to transcend the closed economy model that much more pressing.

Trade Liberalization, Productivity, and Average Real Earnings

A decade ago, Mexico bet that to reverse trends and compete in world markets it had to open its economy. In the aftermath of the macroeconomic stabilization programs implemented in the early 1980s to meet the 1983 debt crisis, the Mexican government embarked on far-reaching economic reforms to transform the very basis of the economy. The main components of this strategy were

- the structural transformation of public finances on both the income and expenditure sides,
- a public debt policy consonant with Mexico's growth perspectives and position in international capital markets,

- liberalization of the implicit or explicit regulatory environment,[3] and
- measures to weaken the anti-export bias that had character-ized the existing relative price system.

This last part of the reform strategy has been an important compo-nent of the policies introduced in Mexico during the past decade. Four of these changes were

- a unilateral tariff reduction that decreased the average Mexican tariff from 25 percent in 1985 to 10 percent in 1988 (figure 3.1);
- Mexico's joining the General Agreement on Tariffs and Trade (GATT) in 1988;
- Mexico's starting to negotiate NAFTA 2 years later; and
- an additional tariff decrease of 5 percent since 1994, when NAFTA came into effect.

The prima facie consequences of this change in strategy have been staggering. Over the past decade, both exports and imports have grown at approximately the same annual rate (16.3 percent), more than six times that of real GDP (2.5 percent). While the overall productivity index grew at rates comparable to the previous period (1.7 percent), there is a clear reversal in manufacturing, particularly in nonmetallic minerals; textiles, clothing, and leather; basic metal industries; and wood and wood products (table 3.4).

We should also note that productivity rates of growth started con-verging, particularly in the manufacturing sector, where their standard deviation fell almost 30 percent. In the labor case, however, dispersion increased more than 40 percent for the economy as a whole and almost 55 percent for the manufacturing sector.

The overall performance reflects an increase in labor productivity (see table 3.5) at levels comparable to the ones existing previously, with the exception of sectors like the textiles, clothing, and leather or the basic metal industries where the absolute value of the reversal is more than 7 percentage points. In the latter case, this performance probably reflects the fact that the capital labor ratio more than doubled between 1988 and 1994 (see figure 3.2).

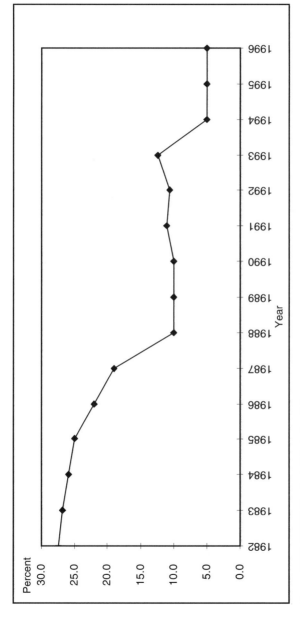

Figure 3.1. Average Mexican Tariff

Source: INEGI, SECOFI, Diseño de Estrategias, S.C.

49

Table 3.4. Total Productivity, 1993 Prices
(Average Annual Percentage Growth)

Sectors	1988–1994
2. Mining	2.75%
3. Manufacturing industry	3.15
3.1 Food, beverages, and tobacco	0.37
3.2 Textiles, clothing, leather	6.02
3.3 Wood and wood products	5.57
3.4 Printing	4.45
3.5 Chemical, petroleum derivates, plastics	1.71
3.6 Nonmetallic minerals, except oil products	6.98
3.7 Basic metal industries	5.58
3.8 Machinery and equipment	3.76
3.9 Others	3.54
4. Construction	1.99
5. Electricity, water, gas	0.48
6. Retailing, restaurants, hotels	2.84
7. Transportation, communications	2.67
8. Financial services	–0.58
9. Government services	–3.06
Total	1.70
Standard Deviation Across Sectors	3.89
Standard Deviation in the Manufacturing Sector	3.12

Sources: INEGI, Banco de México, Diseño de Estrategias S.C.

Table 3.5. Labor Productivity, 1993 Prices
(Average Annual Percentage Growth)

Sectors	1988–1994
2. Mining	2.55%
3. Manufacturing industry	2.93
3.1 Food, beverages, and tobacco	2.78
3.2 Textiles, clothing, leather	3.69
3.3 Wood and wood products	2.28
3.4 Printing	2.52
3.5 Chemical, petroleum derivates, plastics	1.17
3.6 Nonmetallic minerals, except oil products	2.93
3.7 Basic metal industries	13.55
3.8 Machinery and equipment	3.52
3.9 Others	–1.64
4. Construction	–2.07
5. Electricity, water, gas	1.31
6. Retailing, restaurants, hotels	0.08
7. Transportation, communications	1.16
8. Financial services	2.66
9. Government services	–0.41
Total	0.45
Standard Deviation Across Sectors	2.54
Standard Deviation in the Manufacturing Sector	4.49

Sources: INEGI, Banco de México, Diseño de Estrategias S.C.

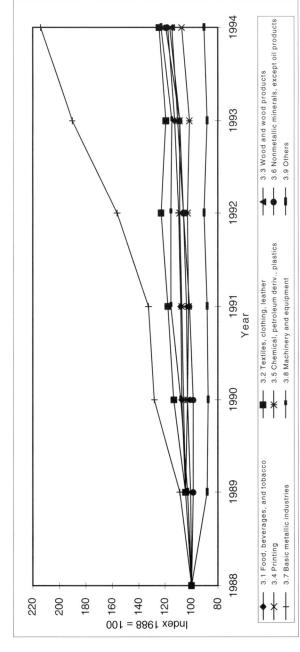

Figure 3.2. Capital per Employee Manufacturing Industry[a]

Legend:
- 3.1 Food, beverages, and tobacco
- 3.4 Printing
- 3.7 Basic metallic industries
- 3.2 Textiles, clothing, leather
- 3.5 Chemical, petroleum deriv., plastics
- 3.8 Machinery and equipment
- 3.3 Wood and wood products
- 3.6 Nonmetallic minerals, except oil products
- 3.9 Others

Index 1988 = 100

Year

[a]1993 prices.
Source: INEGI, Banco de México, Diseño de Estrategias, S.C.

The most significant reversal occurs in the productivity of capital; while it had been decreasing during the previous 17 years, it grew at 2.3 percent a year during 1988–1994, accelerating even more in nonmetallic minerals; textiles, clothing, and leather; and wood and wood products. Furthermore, the dispersion in capital productivity indexes decreased 16 percent for the economy as a whole and 40 percent for the manufacturing industry (see table 3.6).

Table 3.6. Productivity of Capital, 1993 Prices
(Average Annual Percentage Growth)

Sectors	1988–1994
2. Mining	3.24%
3. Manufacturing industry	3.27
3.1 Food, beverages, and tobacco	−0.60
3.2 Textiles, clothing, leather	7.41
3.3 Wood and wood products	6.88
3.4 Printing	5.76
3.5 Chemical, petroleum derivates, plastics	2.07
3.6 Nonmetallic minerals, except oil products	8.25
3.7 Basic metal industries	2.50
3.8 Machinery and equipment	3.93
3.9 Others	6.06
4. Construction	7.79
5. Electricity, water, gas	0.07
6. Retailing, restaurants, hotels	3.94
7. Transportation, communications	3.47
8. Financial services	−1.11
9. Government services	−5.21
Total	2.27
Standard Deviation Across Sectors	5.02
Standard Deviation in the Manufacturing Sector	4.21

Sources: INEGI, Banco de México, Diseño de Estrategias, S.C.

As Romer, Grossman, Helpman, Barro and Sala-i-Martin have suggested, opening an economy increases the variety of capital inputs available to producers, which in turn increases the productivity of capital. As will be seen in the next section, in fact, imports of such goods increased during the first part of this period.

Additional figures at the end of this chapter (figures 3.24–3.29) show the three types of productivity indexes for each sector, as well as for each manufacturing industry, using 1993 prices. While I used data with

1980 prices to measure productivity behavior during 1970–1987, I prefer the series using 1993 prices for the later period because the structure of the economy has changed radically over the past 25 years.

In contradistinction to what happened when the economy was closed, by 1994 all sectors but two (financial services and government services) witnessed increases in both total productivity and capital productivity. In the case of manufacturing, the total productivity of all but two sectors increased more than 20 percent and capital productivity grew more than 50 percent in three of them.

The productivity indexes previously shown cannot be calculated after 1994 because capital stock data are not available. Thus, to evaluate the effects of NAFTA on productivity, one must rely on monthly data that has been published by *Instituto Nacional de Estadística Geografía e Informática* (INEGI) since 1993. Such data can be used to calculate labor productivity and real earnings in the manufacturing industry, while distinguishing between tradable goods sectors (chemicals, basic metal industries, and machinery and equipment) and nontradable goods sectors (food, beverages, and tobacco; wood and wood product; paper and paper products; and nonmetallic minerals) using the exports to GDP ratio (see figures 3.3 and 3.4).[4]

Productivity has grown briskly in the tradable goods sectors as well as in the textiles, clothing, and leather sector (see figures 3.5 through 3.8).[5] The behavior in that sector probably reflects the fact that the capital labor ratio grew almost 25 percent between 1988 and 1994 and that exports of clothing to the United States have grown more than 60 percent since 1990. Likewise, exports of textiles increased more than 50 percent a year after 1994 whereas they were growing at 2.5 percent a year before NAFTA (Hinojosa-Ojeda et al., 1996).

In contradistinction, productivity growth in sectors producing nontradable goods—food, beverages, and tobacco (see figure 3.9); wood and wood products (see figure 3.10); printing (see figure 3.11); and nonmetallic minerals (see figure 3.12)—has been lagging.[6]

In all sectors—producers of tradable and nontradable goods alike—the gap between productivity and real average earnings has grown over time and has done so faster in the tradable goods sector. The excess supply of unskilled labor and recent macroeconomic imbalances, which

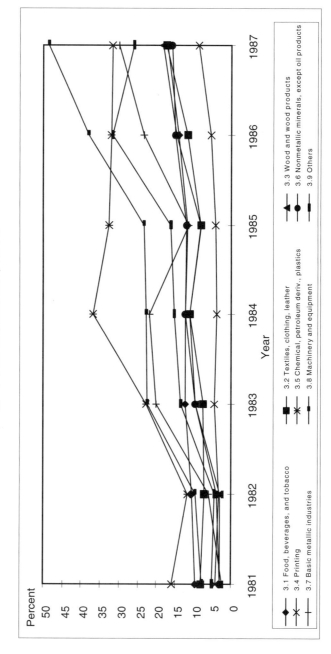

Figure 3.3. Exports/GDP, 1980

3.1 Food, beverages, and tobacco
3.4 Printing
3.7 Basic metallic industries

3.2 Textiles, clothing, leather
3.5 Chemical, petroleum deriv., plastics
3.8 Machinery and equipment

3.3 Wood and wood products
3.6 Nonmetallic minerals, except oil products
3.9 Others

Source: INEGI using 1980 prices.

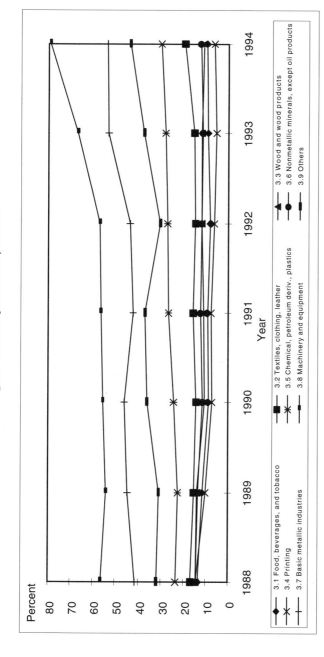

Figure 3.4. Exports/GDP, 1993

Source: INEGI using 1993 prices.

55

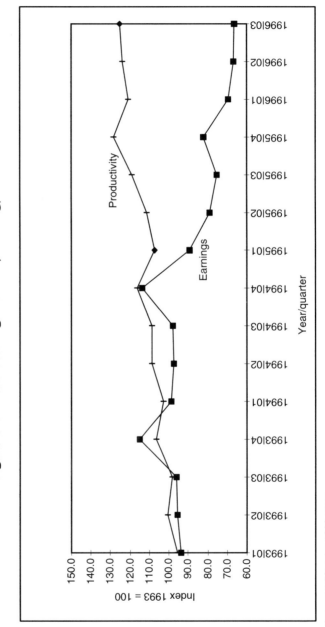

Figure 3.5. Manufacturing—Textiles, Clothing, Leather

Source: INEGI using 1993 prices.

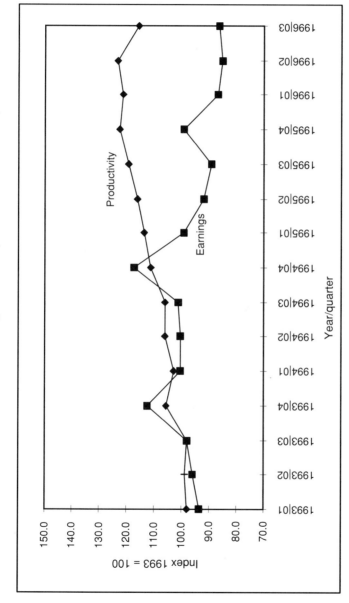

Figure 3.6. Manufacturing—Chemical, Petroleum Derivates, Plastic

Source: INEGI using 1993 prices.

57

Figure 3.7. Manufacturing—Basic Metallic Industries

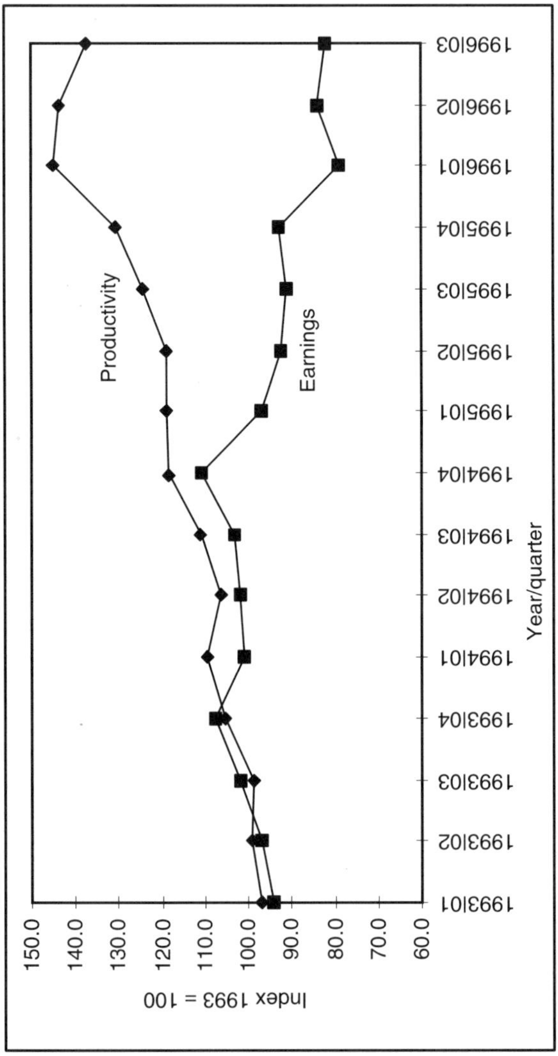

Source: INEGI using 1993 prices.

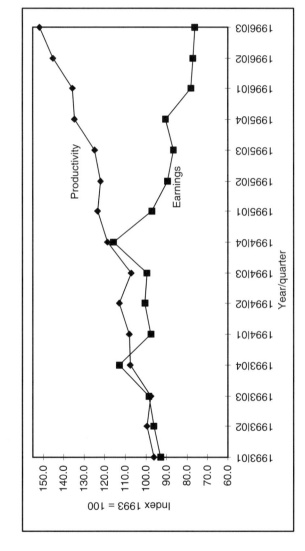

Figure 3.8. Manufacturing—Machinery and Equipment

Source: INEGI using 1993 prices.

Figure 3.9. Manufacturing—Food, Beverages, and Tobacco

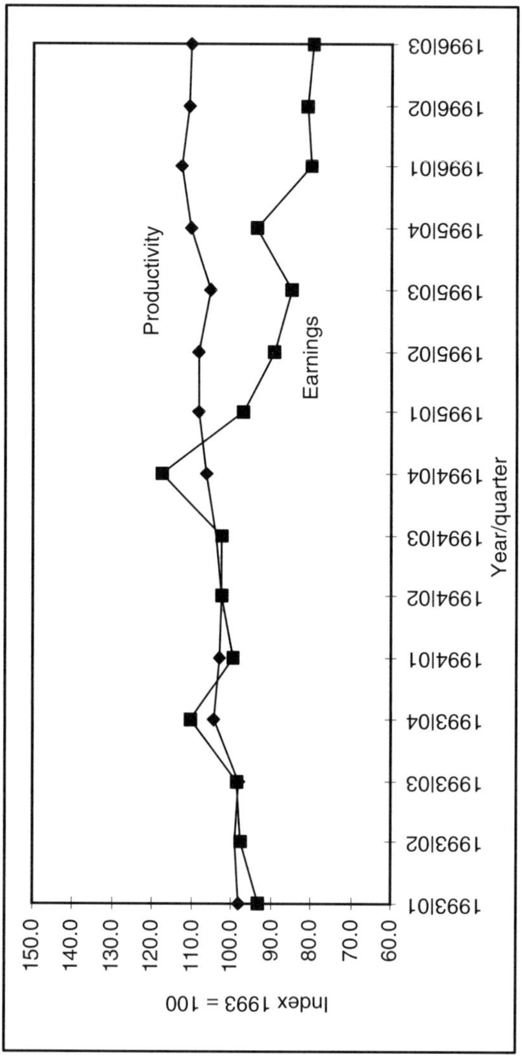

Source: INEGI using 1993 prices.

60

Figure 3.10. Manufacturing—Wood and Wood Products

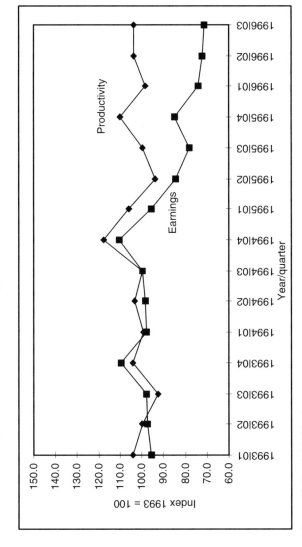

Source: INEGI using 1993 prices.

61

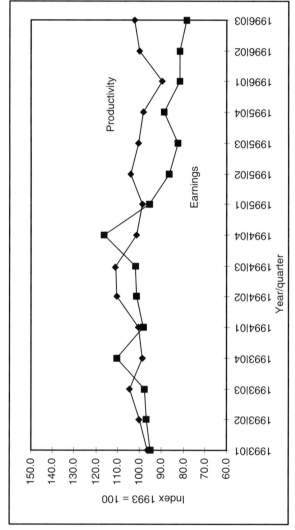

Figure 3.11. Manufacturing—Printing and Paper

Source: INEGI using 1993 prices.

Figure 3.12. Manufacturing—Nonmetallic Minerals, Except Oil Products

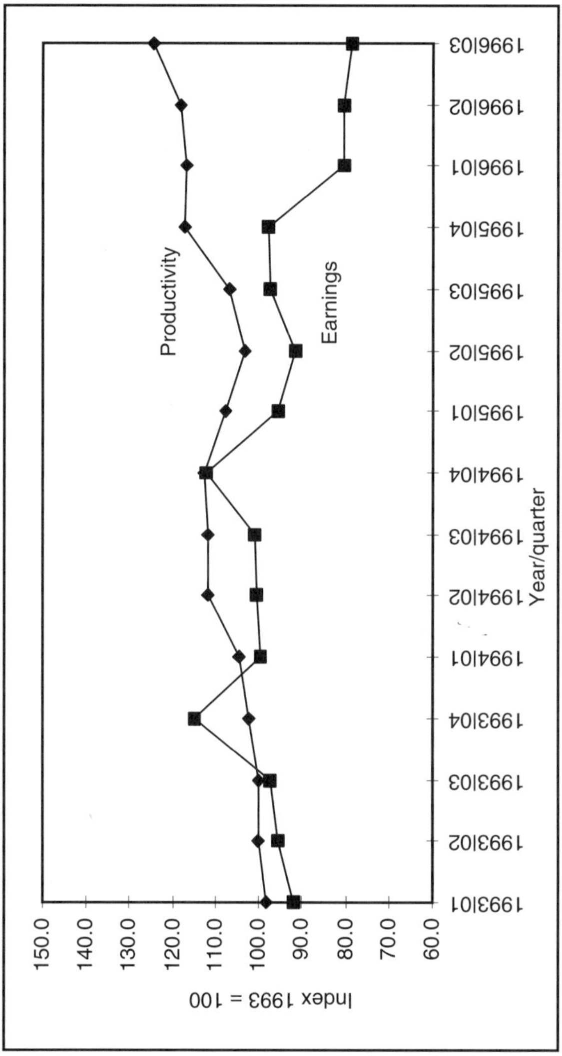

Source: INEGI using 1993 prices.

63

have reflected themselves in both the inflation rate surges and exchange rate devaluations has determined the dynamics of the labor market rather than the productivity increases brought about by international trade liberalization.

Productivity Change and Foreign Trade

Trade liberalization is expected to induce a growth of sectoral productivity both by permitting better access to imported quality intermediate inputs and machinery, and by increasing the pressure on exporting firms to produce at prices and qualities that can compete in world markets. In this section, I will show that this growth is contradicted neither by survey data nor by regression analysis of monthly data for sectoral labor productivity and for exports and imports during 1993–1996.

Between 1986 and 1991, TFP of manufacturing firms that imported intermediate inputs grew at 13.7 percent. TFP of those that imported machinery increased at an annual rate of 9.3 percent. Furthermore, TFP of manufacturing firms that exported part of their production grew more than four times as much as TFP of those that did not.[7]

Conversely, the following regression was estimated:[8]

$$PR_{it} = \alpha_i + \Sigma \beta_{ij} X_{i,t-j} + \Sigma \gamma_{ij} M_{i,t-j} + \varepsilon_{it}$$

where:

PR_{it} = labor productivity in the manufacturing sector i in time t,

X_{it} = Mexican exports of sector i in time t,

M_{it} = Mexican imports of sector i in time t, and

j = 12 lags are estimated.

The results (see table 3.7) suggest that trade liberalization has a significant impact on productivity; imports and exports explain more than 95 percent of the productivity behavior in the tradable goods sectors.[9] Of the 18 estimated coefficients, 12 are significantly different from zero at less than 15 percent marginal significance level; of those 12, 10 have the correct sign while the other 2 indicate a negative influence of imports on productivity.

Table 3.7. Regression Analysis of TFP of Manufacturing, 1993–1996

Sector	R^2	Marginal Significance Level of Q Statistic	Exports	Imports
Food, beverages, and tobacco*	0.937	0.766	-0.185 (.991)	13.150 (.073)
Textiles, clothing, leather	0.974	0.222	0.173 (.119)	.115 (.395)
Wood and wood products	0.926	0.091	2.920 (.003)	0.720 (.027)
Printing*	0.947	0.031	0.008 (.976)	0.132 (.351)
Chemical, petroleum derivates, plastics*	0.983	0.040	0.092 (0.003)	-0.002 (.945)
Nonmetallic minerals, except oil products	0.979	0.557	0.204 (0.012)	-0.369 (0.228)
Basic metal industries*	0.982	0.909	0.176 —	-0.271 (0.060)
Machinery and equipment*	0.990	0.289	0.030 —	-0.028 —
Other manufacturing	0.873	0.128	0.473 (0.033)	0.401 (0.080)

* Cochrane-Orcutt method was used to correct for autoregression of the residuals. Marginal significance levels are in parentheses underneath the coefficient.

Sources: INEGI, SECOFI, and Diseño de Estrategias, S.C.

Regression analysis was also used to evaluate the hypothesis suggested by the previous graphs that sectoral real wages and productivities are not linked. In all cases, the sum of the coefficients of lagged values of productivity on real wages is not statistically different from zero, confirming that trade liberalization has not yet made its effect directly felt on the labor market.

An Evaluation of NAFTA

The 50 percent devaluation of the peso in December 1994, less than 1 year into NAFTA, may have obscured NAFTA's impact on Mexican trade flows and productive restructuring, but it is undeniable that the agreement has strengthened the relationship between its two southernmost partners. Mexican exports to the United States have grown at an average rate of almost 22 percent since the agreement came into effect, compared to less than 13 percent during the previous 3 years.

It has been argued that

> the pattern of U.S.–Mexico trade … began to change nearly
> a decade before NAFTA, with Mexico's unilateral trade liberalization ushering a dramatic growth in the two-way trade
> of intermediate goods, and has not significantly changed
> since the implementation of NAFTA.[10]

In fact, as can be seen in figure 3.13, the share of intermediate goods—net of *maquiladora* imports[11]—in total imports *increased* before the unilateral liberalization of the mid-1980s and *decreased* between 1987 and 1994, after the tariff reduction but before NAFTA. The first round of tariff reductions induced an increase in the importation of capital goods, which may explain the previously mentioned gains in the productivity of capital during 1988–1994.

It is true, nonetheless, that the share of intermediate goods in total imports did increase after NAFTA, suggesting that the agreement *does* represent a change in the way the Mexican and U.S. manufacturing sectors relate to each other, reinforcing their respective comparative advantages more than making them compete with each other.

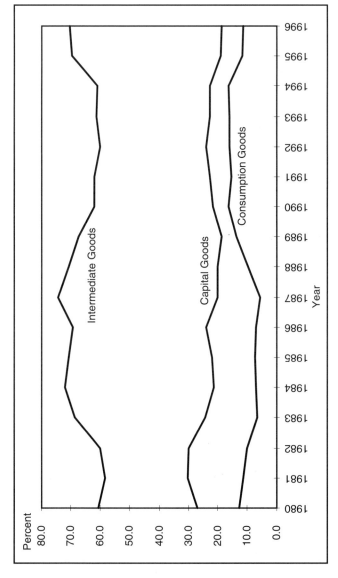

Figure 3.13. Shares of Types of Goods in Imports, 1980–1996

Intermediate Goods

Capital Goods

Consumption Goods

Percent

80.0
70.0
60.0
50.0
40.0
30.0
20.0
10.0
0.0

1980 1981 1982 1983 1984 1985 1986 1987 1988 1989 1990 1991 1992 1993 1994 1995 1996

Year

Sources: Banco de México and Diseño de Estrategias, S.C.

It has also been argued that "Mexican imports have become predominantly linked to the demand for exports rather than fluctuations in Mexican domestic demand."[12]

As I examined this hypothesis, the following regression was estimated using quarterly data for the periods of 1980_I–1987_{IV}, 1988_I–1993_{IV}, and 1994_I–1996_{III}:

$$M_{it} = \alpha + \beta X_{it} + \gamma C_{it} + \delta I_{it} + \zeta RER_{it} + \varepsilon_{it}$$

where:

M_{it} = Mexican imports in sector i at time t,

X_{it} = Mexican exports in sector i at time t,

C_{it} = Mexican private consumption in sector i at time t,

I_{it} = Mexican investment in sector i at time t, and

RER_{it} = Real exchange rate in sector i at time t.

As figures in table 3.8 show, the data suggest the following:

- Between 1980 and 1993, Mexican imports have been correlated mostly to fluctuations in Mexican domestic demand and *not to the demand for Mexican exports.*

- After the implementation of NAFTA, however, the export coefficient is positive and significantly different from zero.

- While the real exchange rate was not a determinant of imports when the economy was closed (before 1988), it has become a significant variable during the past decade.[13] The fact that ζ—the exchange rate coefficient—is almost two and a half times larger after NAFTA came into effect than it was before can reflect an increasing integration between NAFTA's southernmost partners but may also echo the 95 percent devaluation in late 1994 and early 1995.

After NAFTA, Mexican trade has behaved in a manner that is qualitatively different from its behavior after the mid-1980s unilateral liberalization:

- Two-way trade of intermediate goods has grown, while it had decreased in the previous period.

- Mexican imports are becoming more linked to the demand for exports.

These two factors suggest that the Mexican manufacturing sector is restructuring and is increasingly becoming complementary to the U.S. manufacturing sector rather than competing with it.

Table 3.8. Regression Analysis[a] of Mexican Imports, 1980–1996

Coefficient	1980$_I$–1987$_{IV}$	1988$_I$–1993$_{IV}$	1994$_I$–1996$_{III}$
α	−600.6	132.5	590.8
	(.075)	(.650)	(.082)
β	.15	−.09	.49
	(.328)	(.580)	(.119)
γ	.24	.13	.27
	(.005)	(.194)	(.048)
δ	.44	.36	−.25
	(.004)	(.005)	(.250)
ζ	−6,460.6	−13,157.6	−32,459.0
	(.161)	(.003)	(.005)
R^2	.93	.95	.97
Q	7.87	6.12	5.33
	(.929)	(.865)	(.376)

[a]The Cochrane-Orcutt method was used to correct for autoregression of the residuals. Marginal significance levels are shown in parentheses.

Complementarities in Manufacturing Across the Border: Is Mexican Industry Becoming a Large *Maquiladora*?

As can be seen in table 3.9, employment in the manufacturing sector has fared badly since the unilateral opening of the Mexican economy. It decreased 13.5 percent during the first round of liberalization, between 1988 and 1993, and it decreased an additional 4.8 percent since the implementation of NAFTA.

In turn, *maquiladora* employment increased almost 150 percent over the same periods, representing about one-third of total manufacturing employment at the end of 1996. Nonetheless, U.S. Census Bureau data show that Mexican exports under the 9802 regime[14] grew at an average annual rate of 11.5 percent between 1991 and 1995, reinforcing the impression that products are being shipped back and forth with increasing levels of value added (Hinojosa-Ojeda et al., 1996).[15]

Table 3.9. Growth in Manufacturing Employment

	Non-*Maquiladora*	*Maquiladora*
1988–1993[a]	−13.5%	65.9%
1994–1996[b]	−4.8%	48.5%

[a]129 industrial classes.
[b]205 industrial classes.
Source: INEGI Monthly Industrial Survey.

An analysis of sectoral data reveals that production in three sectors—electronics, transportation equipment, and machinery—increasingly consists of assembly of components produced on both sides of the border. Indeed, for the past 6 years, these sectors have accounted for the following:

- more than 60 percent of Mexican manufactured exports to the United States,
- 50 percent of the U.S. exports to Mexico, and
- a rate of growth of exports from Mexico to the United States that almost tripled from about 10 percent during 1990–1993 to about 30 percent during 1993–1996.

Thus, Mexico's restructuring of its industries, which is signified by expansion of *maquiladoras* and behavior of the aforementioned sectors, is the result of strengthening its ties with U.S. industry rather than competing.

Reinforcing these arguments is the fact that manufacturing is increasingly moving to the northern (Norte) and central (Bajío) states that are closer to the United States, to the detriment of the Federal District (D.F.) and the southern (Sur) region. As can be seen in figures 3.14–3.17, the share of total GDP generated in the former regions is growing while the share of the latter ones is falling.[16]

Figure 3.14. Regional Distribution of Manufacuring Industry

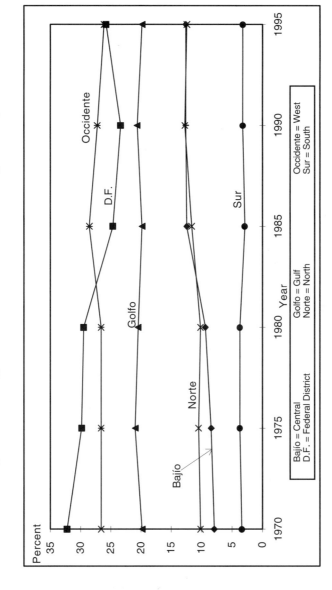

Source: INEGI, Diseño de Estrategias, S.C.

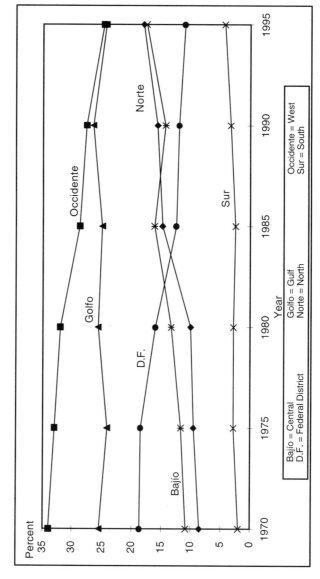

Figure 3.15. Nonmetallic Minerals, Except Oil Products

Source: INEGI, Diseño de Estrategias, S.C.

Figure 3.16. Basic Metallic Industries

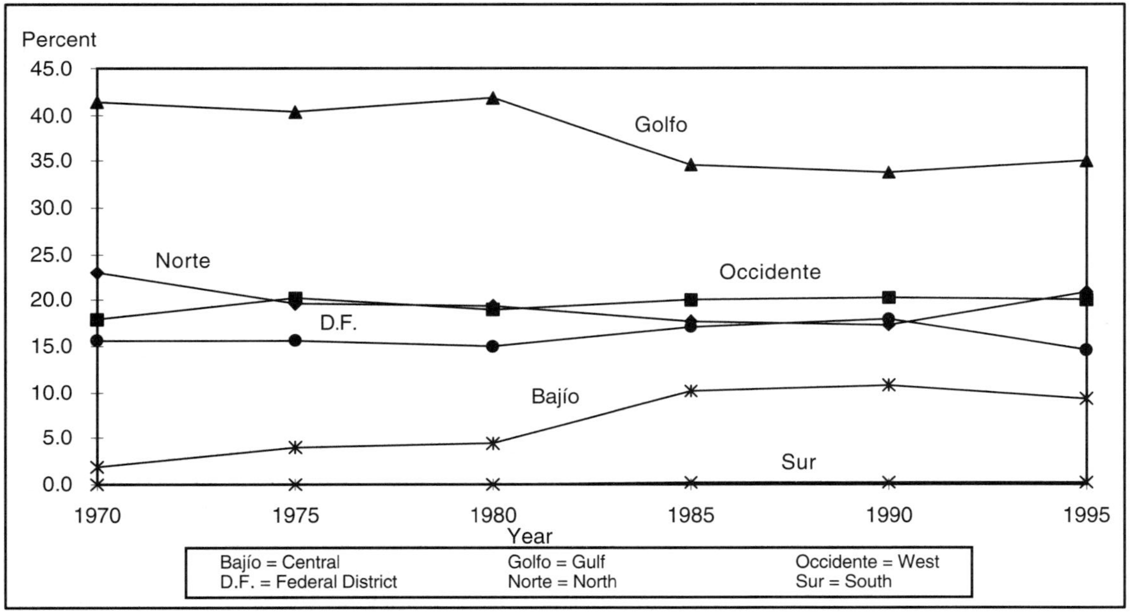
Percent
45.0
40.0
35.0
30.0
25.0
20.0
15.0
10.0
5.0
0.0
1970
1975
1980
1985
1990
1995
Year
Golfo
Norte
Occidente
D.F.
Bajío
Sur
Bajío = Central
D.F. = Federal District
Golfo = Gulf
Norte = North
Occidente = West
Sur = South

Source: INEGI, Diseño de Estrategias, S.C.

Figure 3.17. Machinery and Equipment

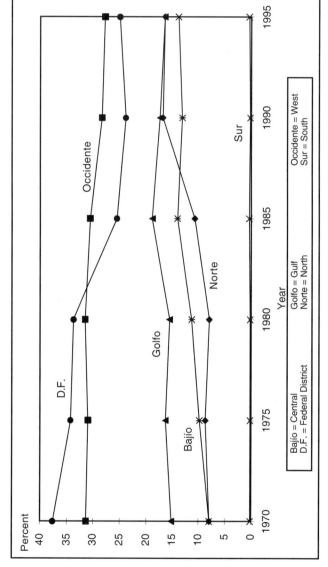

Source: INEGI, Diseño de Estrategias, S.C.

Further consideration of the industries producing tradable goods shows that the Gulf (Golfo) and western (Occidente) regions have also lost importance to the Norte and the Bajío.

Information released by *Secretaría de Comercio y Fomento Industrial* (SECOFI) shows that the number of exporting firms, while small, has grown more than 40 percent since the implementation of NAFTA and that the average amount exported per firm has remained the same, at close to $2 million per firm per year (see table 3.10). Furthermore, while the average amount exported by firm in the tradable goods sectors is larger than the amount exported by their counterparts in the nontradable goods sectors, those amounts have not changed significantly. Thus, the export culture is spreading throughout the manufacturing sector.

Conclusions

The evidence presented in this paper shows that, in the Mexican case, trade liberalization did have a significant impact on productivity, as follows:

- The unilateral liberalization of the 1980s caused a turnaround in the behavior of TFP that reflected an average increase in the productivity of capital in the manufacturing sector of 5.8 percent a year, after it had been stagnant for more than a decade. This increase in capital productivity probably reflects the increased variety of capital inputs available to producers brought about by opening an economy, which then increases the productivity of capital (the Romer-Grossman-Helpman-Barro-Sala-i-Martin effect).
- After NAFTA, labor productivity increased between 20 percent and 40 percent in the tradable goods sectors, while it had little impact in the nontradable goods sectors.

Real earnings have not followed suit. In all sectors, the gap between productivity and real earnings has grown over time and has done so faster in the tradable goods sector. Macroeconomic factors, and not sectoral productivity, seem to determine real earnings.

Table 3.10. Exporting Firms

Sector	1994		1995		1996	
	Number of Firms	Value of Exports	Number of Firms	Value of Exports	Number of Firms	Value of Exports
Food, beverages, and tobacco	2,173	1,641	2,724	2,491	1,586	1,757
Textiles, clothing, leather	2,604	2,662	3,993	3,922	4,878	5,107
Wood and wood products	1,139	499	1,617	483	2,244	701
Printing	1,403	463	1,677	690	1,894	702
Chemical, petroleum derivates, plastics	3,009	3,495	3,841	4,832	4,376	4,731
Nonmetallic minerals, except oil products	1,438	796	1,956	926	2,445	1,006
Basic metal industries	842	1,527	1,093	3,266	993	1,599
Machinery and equipment	6,572	28,230	8,363	34,019	8,927	37,617
Other manufacturing	2,848	2,268	3,404	2,666	3,817	3,512
Total	22,028	41,581	28,668	53,295	31,160	56,732

Sources: SECOFI and Diseño de Estrategias S.C. Exports in millions of dollars.

NAFTA has had two effects on Mexican imports. It has made them more reactive to exchange rate movements, and it has made them dependent on exports, suggesting the appearance of productive complementarities between the Mexican and U.S. manufacturing sectors.

The Mexican manufacturing sector is increasingly reorganizing itself into two groups:

- One group produces tradable goods in a closer and closer relationship with plants located in the United States, where productivity grows. The electronics, transportation equipment, and machinery sectors are canonical in this sense. This growth in productivity implies that GDP is increasingly being produced in regions that have lower transport costs to the United States.
- The other group produces goods for the domestic market, which is still lagging behind.

The challenge Mexico now faces is to strengthen the connections between these two sectors. The preliminary evidence about exporting firms offers a note of hope in that respect. It will be a long time, however, before these phenomena have an impact on the labor market and significantly affect the income distribution or poverty levels.

Figure 3.18. Total Productivity[a]

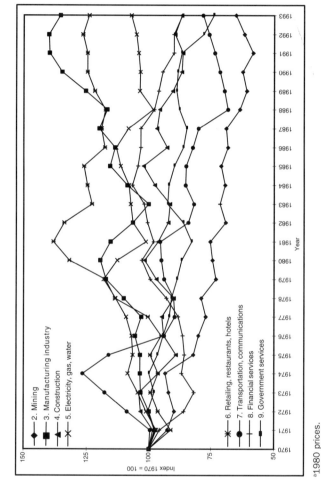

Index 1970 = 100

Year

2. Mining
3. Manufacturing industry
4. Construction
5. Electricity, gas, water

6. Retailing, restaurants, hotels
7. Transportation, communications
8. Financial services
9. Government services

[a]1980 prices.
Source: INEGI, Banco de México, Diseño de Estrategias, S.C.

Figure 3.19. Labor Productivity[a]

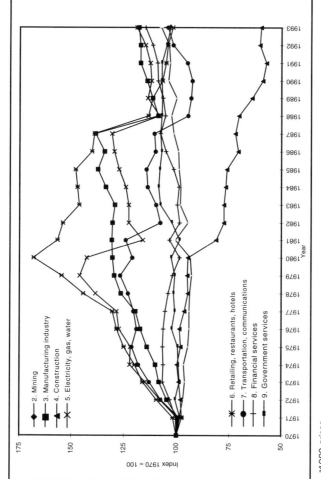

Index 1970 = 100

Year

- ◆ 2. Mining
- ■ 3. Manufacturing industry
- ▲ 4. Construction
- ✕ 5. Electricity, gas, water
- ✳ 6. Retailing, restaurants, hotels
- ● 7. Transportation, communications
- ╬ 8. Financial services
- ■ 9. Government services

[a]1980 prices.
Source: INEGI, Banco de México, Diseño de Estrategias, S.C.

Figure 3.20. Productivity of Capital[a]

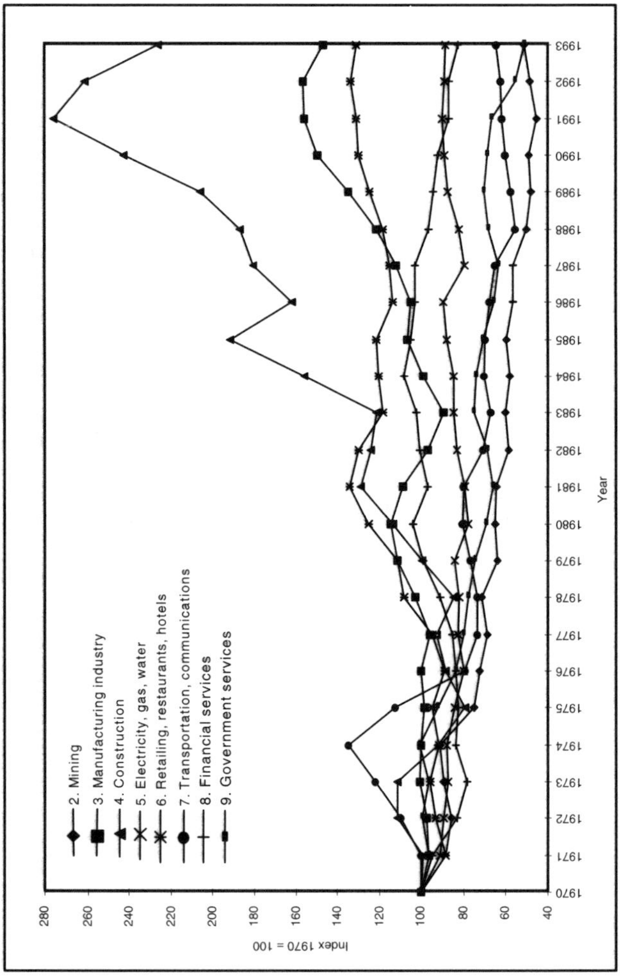
2. Mining
3. Manufacturing industry
4. Construction
5. Electricity, gas, water
6. Retailing, restaurants, hotels
7. Transportation, communications
8. Financial services
9. Government services
Index 1970 = 100
280
260
240
220
200
180
160
140
120
100
80
60
40
1970
1971
1972
1973
1974
1975
1976
1977
1978
1979
1980
1981
1982
1983
1984
1985
1986
1987
1988
1989
1990
1991
1992
1993
Year

[a]1980 prices.
Source: INEGI, Banco de México, Diseño de Estrategias, S.C.

Figure 3.21. Total Productivity—Manufacturing Industry[a]

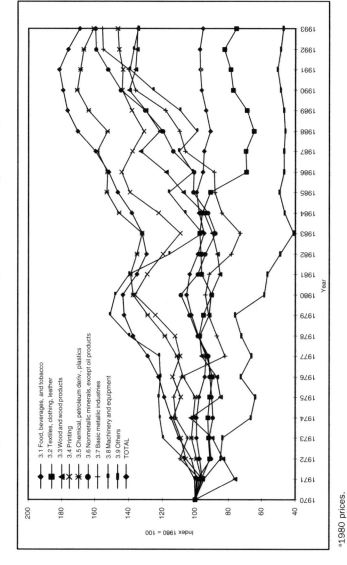

3.1 Food, beverages, and tobacco
3.2 Textiles, clothing, leather
3.3 Wood and wood products
3.4 Printing
3.5 Chemical, petroleum deriv., plastics
3.6 Nonmetallic minerals, except oil products
3.7 Basic metallic industries
3.8 Machinery and equipment
3.9 Others
TOTAL

Index 1980 = 100

Year

[a]1980 prices.
Source: INEGI, Banco de México, Diseño de Estrategias, S.C.

Figure 3.22. Labor Productivity—Manufacturing Industry[a]

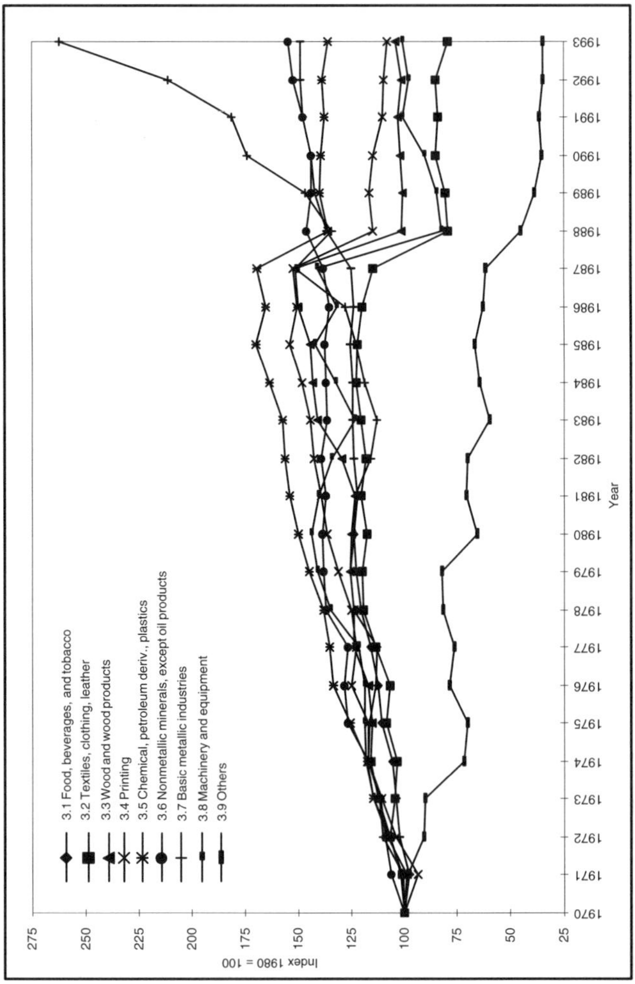
3.1 Food, beverages, and tobacco
3.2 Textiles, clothing, leather
3.3 Wood and wood products
3.4 Printing
3.5 Chemical, petroleum deriv., plastics
3.6 Nonmetallic minerals, except oil products
3.7 Basic metallic industries
3.8 Machinery and equipment
3.9 Others
Index 1980 = 100
275
250
225
200
175
150
125
100
75
50
25
1970
1971
1972
1973
1974
1975
1976
1977
1978
1979
1980
1981
1982
1983
1984
1985
1986
1987
1988
1989
1990
1991
1992
1993
Year

[a]1980 prices.
Source: INEGI, Banco de México, Diseño de Estrategias, S.C.

Figure 3.23. Productivity of Capital—Manufacturing Industry[a]

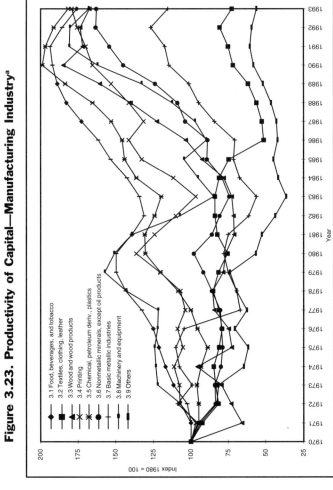

3.1 Food, beverages, and tobacco
3.2 Textiles, clothing, leather
3.3 Wood and wood products
3.4 Printing
3.5 Chemical, petroleum deriv., plastics
3.6 Nonmetallic minerals, except oil products
3.7 Basic metallic industries
3.8 Machinery and equipment
3.9 Others

Index 1980 = 100

Year

[a]1980 prices.
Source: INEGI, Banco de México, Diseño de Estrategias, S.C.

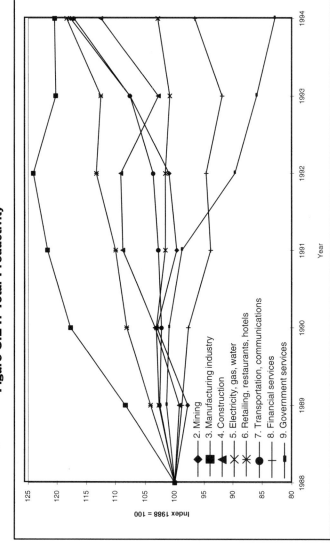

Figure 3.24. Total Productivity[a]

[a]1993 prices.

Source: INEGI, Banco de México, Diseño de Estrategias, S.C.

84

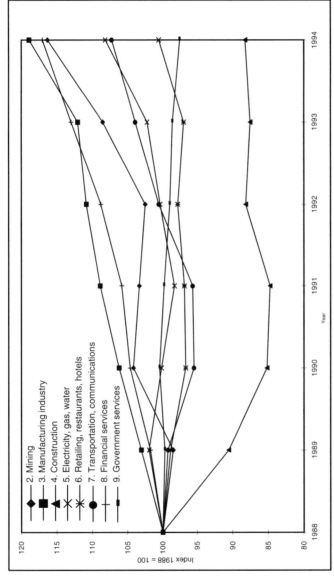

Figure 3.25. Labor Productivity[a]

2. Mining
3. Manufacturing industry
4. Construction
5. Electricity, gas, water
6. Retailing, restaurants, hotels
7. Transportation, communications
8. Financial services
9. Government services

Index 1988 = 100

Year

[a]1993 prices.
Source: INEGI, Banco de México, Diseño de Estrategias, S.C.

85

Figure 3.26. Productivity of Capital[a]

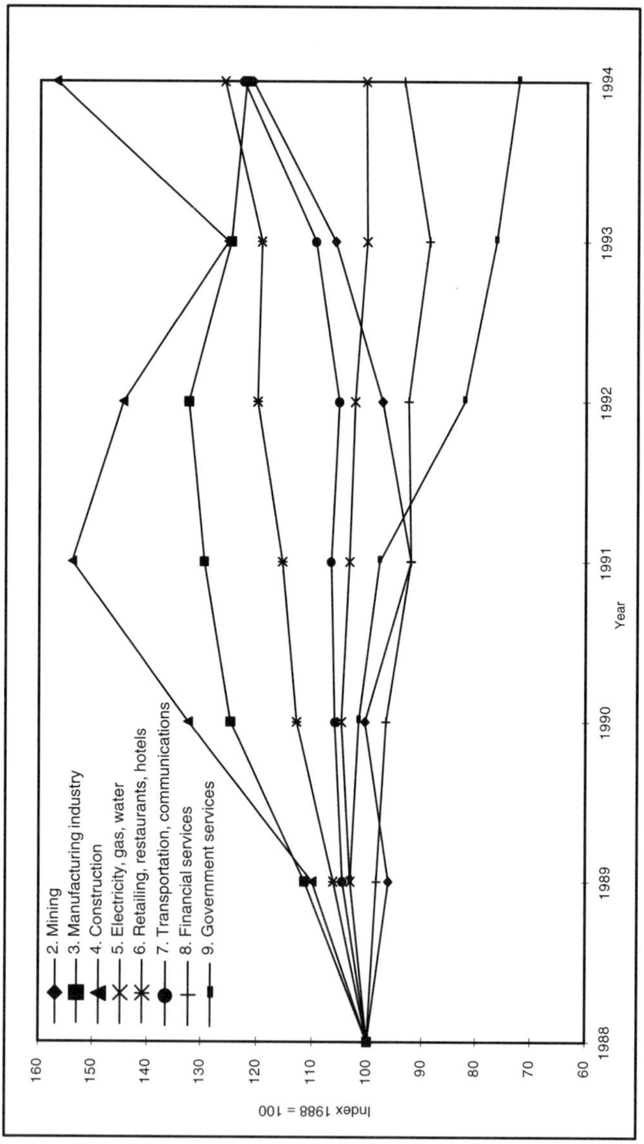

2. Mining
3. Manufacturing industry
4. Construction
5. Electricity, gas, water
6. Retailing, restaurants, hotels
7. Transportation, communications
8. Financial services
9. Government services
Index 1988 = 100
160
150
140
130
120
110
100
90
80
70
60
1988
1989
1990
1991
1992
1993
1994
Year

[a]1993 prices.
Source: INEGI, Banco de México, Diseño de Estrategias, S.C.

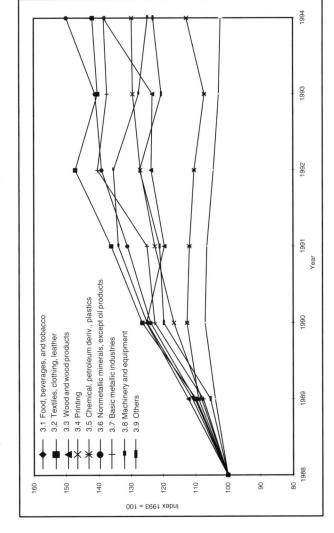

Figure 3.27. Total Productivity—Manufacturing Industry[a]

3.1 Food, beverages, and tobacco
3.2 Textiles, clothing, leather
3.3 Wood and wood products
3.4 Printing
3.5 Chemical, petroleum deriv., plastics
3.6 Nonmetallic minerals, except oil products
3.7 Basic metallic industries
3.8 Machinery and equipment
3.9 Others

Index 1993 = 100

Year

[a]1993 prices.
Source: INEGI, Banco de México, Diseño de Estrategias, S.C.

Figure 3.28. Labor Productivity—Manufacturing Industry[a]

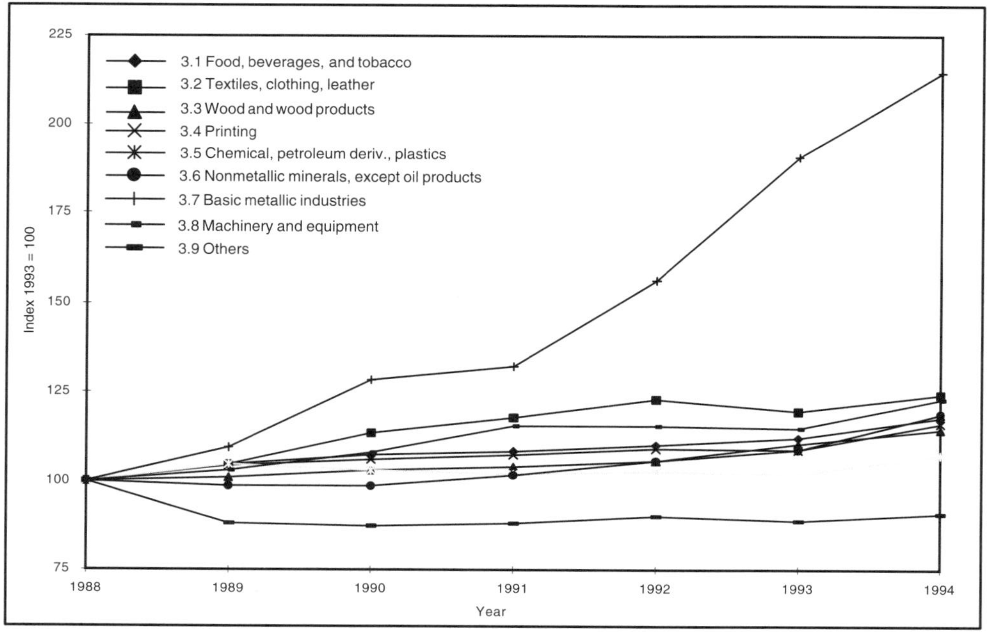

Legend:
- ◆ 3.1 Food, beverages, and tobacco
- ■ 3.2 Textiles, clothing, leather
- ◀ 3.3 Wood and wood products
- ✕ 3.4 Printing
- ✱ 3.5 Chemical, petroleum deriv., plastics
- ● 3.6 Nonmetallic minerals, except oil products
- ┼ 3.7 Basic metallic industries
- ▮ 3.8 Machinery and equipment
- ▬ 3.9 Others

Index 1993 = 100

Year

[a]1993 prices.
Source: INEGI, Banco de México, Diseño de Estrategias, S.C.

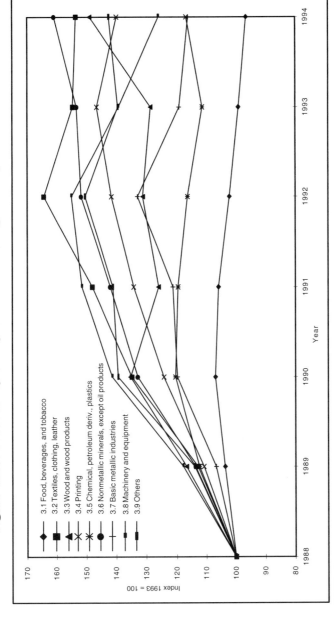

Figure 3.29. Productivity of Capital—Manufacturing Industry[a]

3.1 Food, beverages, and tobacco
3.2 Textiles, clothing, leather
3.3 Wood and wood products
3.4 Printing
3.5 Chemical, petroleum deriv., plastics
3.6 Nonmetallic minerals, except oil products
3.7 Basic metallic industries
3.8 Machinery and equipment
3.9 Others

Index 1993 = 100

Year

[a]1993 prices.
Source: INEGI, Banco de México, Diseño de Estrategias, S.C.

89

Endnotes

[1] During the 1970s, Mexico established a program to stimulate employment that permits duty-free import of intermediate inputs and machinery of *maquiladoras* as long as the final product is exported after processing. The original intent was to curtail undocumented migration to the United States by creating employment, initially in border areas; since then the program has been extended to the whole country.

[2] All calculations were done by Diseño de Estrategias with *Instituto Nacional de Estadística Geografía e Informática* (INEGI) and *Banco de México* data. On the whole, these results reproduce the work of Enrique Hernández Laos, *Tendencias de la Productividad en México (1970–1991), Secretaría del Trabajo y Previsión Social* (STPS), 1994, while correcting minor mistakes and extending the time period.

[3] Gradual elimination of price controls, along with restrictions on foreign investment, privatization of state-owned enterprises, growth of flexibility in the labor market, etcetera.

[4] Data used are from the INEGI databanks.

[5] The rates of growth were 23.3 percent for the textiles, clothing, and leather sector; 20.1 percent for the chemical, petroleum derivates, and plastic sector; 42.0 percent for the basic metallic industries sector; and 44.0 percent for the machinery and equipment sector.

[6] The rates of growth were 11.4 percent for the food, beverages, and tobacco sector; 1.9 percent for the wood and wood products sector; −2.5 percent for the printing sector; and 19.6 percent for the nonmetallic minerals sector, except for oil products.

[7] See Enrique Hernández Laos (1994).

[8] Monthly data for the 1993–1996 period were obtained from INEGI and SECOFI.

[9] The value of the Q statistic indicates that the residuals are not white noise in more than half of the estimated equations.

[10] See Hinojosa-Ojeda et al. (1996).

[11] As of January 1991, INEGI data on intermediate imports include *maquiladora* imports that were not previously included.

[12] See INEGI data.

[13] This statement confirms the results in Graf-Noriega (1996).

[14] The 9802 allows re-entry of U.S. components assembled in Mexico free of tariffs.

[15] There exist significant data problems, however, that prevent us from establishing a clear picture. Furthermore, as trade between Mexico and the United States is liberalized, trade statistics will tend to underestimate cross-border manufacturing linkages. There will be no reason to continue registration in the program as administrative costs will be larger than the benefits derived from the program.

[16] *Bajío* (Central): Aguascalientes, Guanajuato, Hidalgo, Morelos, San Luis Potosí, Tlaxcala, Querétaro, Zacatecas; *Golfo* (Gulf): Nuevo León, Puebla, Tabasco, Tamaulipas, Veracruz; *D.F.* (Federal District): Distrito Federal; *Norte* (North): Baja California Norte, Coahuila, Chihuahua, Durango, Michoacán, Sonora; *Occidente* (West): Baja California Sur, Colima, Estado de México, Jalisco, Nayarit, Sinaloa; *Sur* (South): Campeche, Chiapas, Guerrero, Oaxaca, Quintana Roo, Yucatán.

Bibliography

Barro, Robert, J. and Xavier Sala-i-Martin. *Economic Growth.* McGraw Hill, 1995.

Graf-Noriega, Juan Pablo. *El Crecimiento de las Exportaciones y el Desempeño de la Productividad en la Industria Manufacturera en México.* Mexico, D.F.: Banco de México, 1996.

Grossman, Gene M. and Elhanan Helpman. *Innovation and Growth in the Global Economy.* MIT Press, London, 1991.

Hernández Laos, Enrique. *Tendencias de la Productividad en México (1970–1991).* Mexico, D.F.: Secretaria del Trabajo y Previsión Social. 1994.

Hinojosa-Ojeda, et al. *North American Integration Three Years after NAFTA : A Framework for Tracking , Modeling and Internet Accessing the National and Regional Labor Market Impacts.* UCLA, NAID Center, December 1996.

Romer, Paul M. "Idea Gaps and Object Gaps in Economic Development", *Journal of Monetary Economics*, 32, December, 1993.

CHAPTER 4

Comments on Chapters 1, 2, and 3

Steven M. Beckman
United Auto Workers

While measures of productivity in the past 20 years have shown only small increases overall, real wages have failed to keep up in the United States. This difference has left workers with less job security, less income, and an uncertainty about how to improve their economic situation in the future.

What is the role of the North American Free Trade Agreement (NAFTA) and the economic integration process in creating this reality for American workers? This question, of course, is not a simple one, but there are some obvious ways to look at it.

The view of the United Auto Workers (UAW) is that NAFTA reinforced a process of industrial restructuring that first took place in the United States, was propelled in Canada by the Free Trade Agreement (FTA), and was extended to Mexico in 1986 with accession of General Agreement on Tariffs and Trade (GATT). As a result, real wages in manufacturing in the United States peaked around 1985. Similar breaks occurred in Canada and Mexico around the same time.

Manufacturing productivity continued to increase during the past decade despite the lethargy in real wages. As a result, the disconnect between workers' incomes and productivity, as reflected in the public anxiety about job security and living standards, was created.

The papers prepared for this meeting document the gap between productivity growth and compensation for workers in all three NAFTA countries. Given the commitment made by the governments and reinforced by many economists that NAFTA would increase living standards in the region by raising compensation as productivity improved. The findings of the researchers in the three countries—that this has not taken place—are important and telling.

In the U.S. auto industry, real wages peaked earlier than for all manufacturing workers, around 1980, as the industry's restructuring process intensified after the second oil crisis, when imports of vehicles from Japan increased rapidly. Outsourcing of auto parts mushroomed, and U.S. parts companies closed plants in the Midwest and opened new plants in the South and abroad, including many *maquiladora* (in-bond industries located in national territory that establish a contract to process or assemble components and machinery temporarily imported and to re-export them thereafter; by 1988 the *maquiladoras* were allowed to sell a portion of their goods on the domestic market) plants in Mexico. The result was a substantial reduction in unionization, widespread worker dislocation, and far lower production and worker compensation in the industry. Large productivity increases in the U.S. auto industry took place from 1980 to 1985, just as compensation declined. In the past 10 years, productivity gains have come more slowly, but compensation was lower in 1994 than in 1985.

The situation in the Canadian and Mexican auto industries is also of concern to the UAW. After all, the economic integration process in the region includes the integration of this industry. Trade among the three countries in this one industry is huge, accounting for more than a quarter of U.S. trade with Canada and Mexico.

In what are referred to in the United States as the "bad days of import substitution" in Mexico, wages for auto workers, when adjusted for inflation, increased dramatically. Then the 1982 debt crisis occurred, and the adoption of neoliberal policies followed a few years later.

As a result, the real compensation of Mexican auto workers today is half of what it was in 1980. Looking at aggregate data, compensation in 1994 was below the level of 1985, *before* the latest peso devaluation.

Collective bargaining contracts between Mexican auto workers and U.S. multinational producers demonstrate what has happened to workers in the same auto plants over this period and what the restructuring of auto production is doing to the relationship between worker incomes and productivity in the Mexican auto industry.

In Ford's Cuautitlan plant, the 1979 collective bargaining agreement contained a wage range of from 40,000 old pesos per hour to 73,000. If the real value of that pay had been maintained with no improvement for productivity gains, pay in Cuautitlan in 1995 would have been, roughly, from 14 new pesos per hour to 28.[1] Actual pay was from 6 new pesos per hour to 12. The 50 percent decline in real wages for Mexican workers since 1982, which is shown in the aggregate data, is corroborated by the figures for these workers. The lack of any share of the productivity gains for workers makes the compensation loss and the effect on income inequality even greater.

Here is another example of the profound impact of the industry restructuring on Mexican auto worker wages. In 1987, the GM truck plant in Mexico City paid wages of from 6 new pesos per hour to 12 (note that this pay is the same as in Cuautitlan in 1995). The plant closed recently and production moved to a new plant in Silao, Guanajuato. In 1996, the pay in Silao ranged from 4 new pesos to 13 new pesos per hour (only a few workers are at the top of the wage scale). The workers in the Mexico City plant probably had the highest wages for production workers in the auto industry. The workers in Silao make less today, in absolute terms, with no adjustment for the sizable inflation, than workers making similar vehicles around 10 years ago.

The Mexico City plant was old and inefficient; the new plant is modern in every way. Since it opened, virtually all of its production has been exported to the United States, so it is certainly making a world-class product. Not only are the workers in Silao paid substantially less than the workers in Mexico City who preceded them, but also thousands of fewer workers are producing the same volume of output. This fact indicates that the productivity of the workforce has increased dramatically. Again, compensation for the workers and productivity have sharply diverged.

In citing these examples, I have avoided making comparisons in dollars or comparing compensation between Mexican and U.S. workers. The issue here is the buying power of Mexican workers relative to changes in productivity, not to changes in exchange rates or to changes in U.S. worker compensation. Just as American workers' compensation failed to grow with the productivity gains in the 1980s, Mexican workers are failing to obtain a fair share of the large productivity gains that are being generated in the auto industry today.

Is the situation different in other industries that experience regional integration? I would doubt it. Rapid growth in Mexican production is taking place in several export-oriented industries, thereby generating increased output with fewer workers and large productivity gains. The decline in compensation reinforces the problem of maintaining growth in Mexican consumption. That decline is certainly causing problems for American workers competing with an expanding range of products made in Mexico for export.

As I noted at the outset, the findings of researchers—that worker compensation in all three NAFTA countries is lagging behind productivity growth—is important information. The soothing assurances of the elites in all three countries that "free trade" would benefit average citizens can no longer be assumed to be accurate. We now know that the rules, incentives, and structures created by NAFTA, which set the conditions for economic integration among Canada, Mexico, and the United States, do not ensure that workers will benefit from the integration process.

The UAW believes that only changes in NAFTA itself would create the conditions under which workers would benefit from regional integration through higher productivity and higher compensation. We made this argument throughout the negotiation and debate over passage of NAFTA. The task ahead is to develop appropriate mechanisms—in labor–management relationships, in government economic and social policy, and in international trade rules and practices—that will accomplish for working people the improved living standards that have been promised and remain undelivered. NAFTA country gov-

ernments and the institutions created by NAFTA, including the Labor Secretariat, could contribute to this effort, but not if they continue
to defend the inadequate, anti-worker status quo.

Endnotes

[1] Translation note: In 1993, a new currency was adopted in Mexico; the "new peso" is
equivalent to 1,000 old pesos.

CHAPTER 5

Comments on Chapter 2

Andrew Jackson
Canadian Labour Congress

Productivity—the value of the output of goods and services produced per hour worked—is a crucial determinant of national income and wealth. Productivity increases as a result of (1) capital investment (i.e., in buildings, machinery, and equipment); (2) investment in the education and skills of workers; and (3) innovation, growth of knowledge, and technical progress. In the business sector, productivity tends to be highest in the larger scale, capital, and skills-intensive sectors. In Canada, high-productivity sectors tend to be unionized and to pay well above average wages. (Since the output of not-for-profit sectors of the economy is not sold, the value of output is defined as the sum total of inputs, so labor productivity growth is zero by definition.)

Historically, workers have shared in productivity gains through higher wages, shorter work hours, and social programs and public services financed from increased national income. In the 30-odd years between World War II and the mid-1970s, labor productivity rose rapidly. This productivity was quickly translated into rising real wages and, to a lesser degree, into shorter work time. Since the mid-1970s, productivity growth has slowed considerably, and real wage growth has slowed to an even greater degree. Not only has productivity growth slowed, but also a gap has opened between productivity growth and real wage growth.

The growing gap between productivity growth and wage growth has been greater in North America than in Europe and, until very recently, greater in the United States than in Canada. This gap is explained, in significant measure, by the weakening of the bargaining power of labor as compared to that of capital. The decline in worker bargaining power in the labor market is to be seen in declining unionization rates in the business sector and—most important, in Canada, where private sector union density has remained fairly stable—in the erosion of bargaining leverage of unions vis-à-vis employers. The decline in worker bargaining power is evident in the erosion of centralized and pattern bargaining, as well as in the erosion of legislated employment standards such as minimum wages, which have historically reflected labor influence in the political arena.

The result of the growing gap has been a major redistribution of income from labor to capital. In October 1995, the International Monetary Fund (IMF) reported in *World Economic Outlook* that "profit shares (corporate profits as a share of national income) and rates of return on capital in industrial countries in 1994 were the highest in twenty years" (IMF 1995, p.14). According to Organization for Economic Cooperation and Development (OECD) data drawn on by the IMF, the average profit share has risen from about 13 percent of national income to almost 17 percent since 1982, and rates of return on capital have risen by about one-third over the same period.

The ability of capital to win a larger share of a more slowly growing pie is, first and foremost, a result of the end of full employment from the mid-1970s, of the decline in worker bargaining power that has flowed from the high and still rising rates of unemployment, and of the growth of very precarious and unstable forms of employment. Since the mid-1970s, macroeconomic policy in most industrial countries has emphasized low inflation, and high unemployment has been deliberately maintained to dampen the growth of wages. Policy makers generally hold that unemployment should be maintained at or above the

Non-Accelerating Inflation Rate of Unemployment (NAIRU) and that the NAIRU is best lowered through measures to deregulate labor markets. In practice, this philosophy translates into tight monetary and fiscal polices, combined with measures to attack institutions that strengthen the bargaining power of labor—unions, employment standards, and social programs that reduce dependence upon wage income. In Canada, recent years have seen a major undermining of the Unemployment Insurance program—the proportion of unemployed workers who qualify for benefits has fallen from 90 percent to below 50 percent in the 1990s—and unions as institutions have come under attack in some provincial jurisdictions.

Capital Seeks to Restrain Wage Growth

Another factor behind the erosion of workers' bargaining power has been globalization of trade and investment. Increased international trade—most important among the advanced industrial countries—has increased competitive pressures on capital, and it has tended to erode centralized and pattern bargaining arrangements that "took wages out of competition" in the earlier period. Increased trade in manufactured goods with the developing world has added to competitive pressures. Canadian trade overwhelmingly is with the United States and other advanced industrial countries, but there are clearly "knock-on" effects from increased U.S. investment in, and trade with, Mexico both before and after NAFTA. In much more competitive markets, capital has sought to restrain the growth of wage costs and has channeled new investments disproportionately to those locations where wages are low in relation to productivity.

As documented in the recent Canadian Labour Congress (CLC) report on NAFTA (titled *Social Dimensions of North American Economic Integration*), the Canada–U.S. Free Trade Agreement and NAFTA have increased the pressures of international competition on Canadian capital. This increase has resulted in large job losses in the highly exposed and integrated manufacturing sector and in a significant restructuring of the operations that have remained. In the competitive struggle for survival and growth, capital has striven to raise productivity while minimizing wage costs. There has also been a significant outflow of direct and indirect investment capital from Canada to the United States.

In the Canadian context, this restructuring process has taken place in a context of significant macroeconomic slack. The output gap in Canada has been at or near the highest in the OECD area since the late 1980s, and it remains very high. The unemployment rate has never fallen below 9 percent in the 1990s, which is well above most estimates of so-called structural unemployment. (The Department of Finance estimates that the NAIRU is 7.4 percent.)

Monetary tightening by the Bank of Canada from 1989 was explicitly intended to achieve a zero inflation objective. Since 1993, the Bank has had a formal mandate to keep inflation in a range of 1 percent to 3 percent. Monetary tightening was also intended, in part, to discipline Canadian labor as the Free Trade Agreement (FTA) came into effect. In the expansion period that followed the recession of the early 1980s, productivity grew more slowly than in the U.S. manufacturing sector, while real wages grew more strongly. The result was an erosion of competitiveness that was offset by a substantial currency depreciation. Higher union density levels were likely a major factor behind deteriorating cost competitiveness. However, it should be emphasized that the problem for Canadian capital was not that wage growth exceeded productivity growth, but rather that wages increased more rapidly in relation to productivity than they did in the United States.

From 1989 through the early 1990s, the effects of the introduction of the FTA on an already highly integrated and exposed Canadian economy were greatly compounded by a sharp exchange rate appreciation. While the dollar has since fallen, thus restoring cost competitiveness to the traded sector, massive fiscal restraint has produced a deeply depressed domestic economy. In the slow recovery of the 1990s—which has been weaker than in the United States—a "dual economy" has emerged. Export-oriented resource and manufacturing sectors have done well, while domestic sectors, such as retail trade and construction, have fared badly. The public sector—one-fifth of the economy—is being deeply cut back.

What has been the nature of the linkage between productivity and wages in this context?[1] As shown in figure 5.1, real wage growth, or wages deflated by the Consumer Price Index (CPI), for the entire business sector has lagged productivity growth since the mid-1970s, though the gap has recently closed to some degree. The trend to a slowdown in productivity growth is clear, though productivity growth jumped in the expansion period of the late 1980s (indicating the large costs of macroeconomic restraint in terms of efficiency, as well as in terms of lost jobs). As shown in figure 5.2, a similar gap between real wages and productivity opened up in the manufacturing sector from the mid-1970s, and it has recently widened as productivity has grown much more strongly than real wages.

Figures 5.3 and 5.4 look at the more recent period since the FTA and NAFTA came into effect. In the business sector as a whole, after widening during the recession of the early 1990s, the wage to productivity gap has begun to close. This trend has not taken place in the manufacturing sector. Even in the recovery—which, as noted above, has been particularly marked in output terms in the traded sector—the gap between wages and productivity has remained wide. There is clearly some evidence of improved productivity performance in this period.

Chasm Opens Between Productivity and Wage Trends

Table 5.1 adds a bit more detail to this very general picture, showing that nothing less than a chasm has emerged between productivity and wage trends (for production workers only) in some of the most important export-oriented industries.

The evidence clearly shows that the disconnect between wages and productivity is greatest in those sectors most highly exposed to the forces of international competition. In this case, competition is from U.S. manufacturers who operate largely on a nonunion basis, and from Mexico, where standardized and, to a lesser extent, sophisticated industrial production and relatively high productivity can be combined

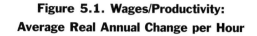

Figure 5.1. Wages/Productivity:
Average Real Annual Change per Hour

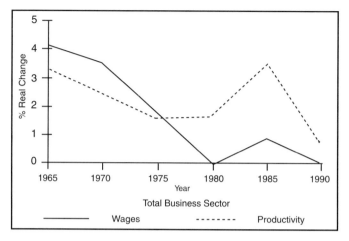

Figure 5.2. Wages/Productivity:
Average Real Annual Change per Hour

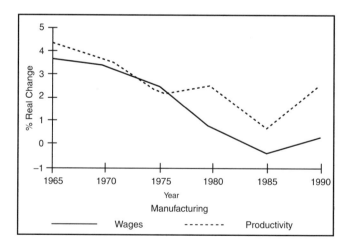

Figure 5.3. Wages/Productivity:
Real Annual Change per Hour

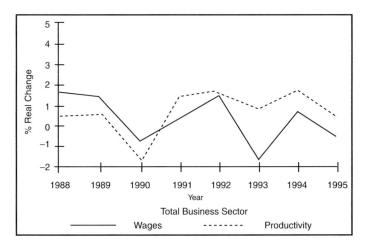

Figure 5.4. Wages/Productivity:
Real Annual Change per Hour

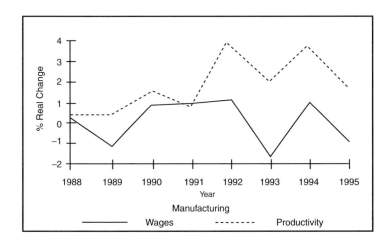

Table 5.1. Productivity and Wages in Selected Industries

	Change in Manufacturing Value Added per Production Worker 1992 to 1994 (percent)	Change in Average Hourly Earnings (hourly paid workers) 1992 to 1994 (percent)
Machinery (except electrical)	14.7	1.9
Electrical and electronic products	24.8	1.6
Transportation equipment industries	28.3	8.4
—Aircraft and parts	30.8	4.6
—Motor vehicles	39.9	13.0
Primary metal industries	35.6	3.1
Paper and allied products	26.1	3.8

Sources: Industry Canada. "Strategies" Database. (Ottowa: Author, 1996).
Statistics Canada. *Annual Estimates of Employment, Earnings, and Hours.* 1996.

with very low wages. Something more than the macroeconomic environment is depressing wages in relation to productivity in the manufacturing sector. Despite the fact that more than 60 percent of production is exported and that the U.S. market has been growing relatively strongly, wages in the integrated sector have grown somewhat less rapidly in relation to productivity than in the business sector as a whole.

According to the Bureau of Labor Statistics (BLS) data (USDL–284), real hourly compensation in both the U.S. manufacturing sector and the Canadian manufacturing sector fell by a total of 0.5 percent between 1992 and 1995. Over this same period, output per hour in manufacturing rose by 11.9 percent in the United States compared to 7.2 percent in Canada. Were it not for exchange rate depreciation, which has driven the recovery, the cost competitiveness of Canadian manufacturers would have been eroded.

Apparently, the continuing very wide gap between productivity growth and wages in the United States is driving the evolution of wages in relation to productivity in Canada. The U.S. gap is likely explained both by institutional factors—the relatively weak bargaining power of labor—and by international competitive factors. A major difference between Canada and the United States is that the unionization rate in Canadian manufacturing is 33.4 percent. It is interesting to note that from 1992 to 1995, again on the basis of BLS data, output per hour in German manufacturing rose by slightly more than in the United States (12.0 percent versus 11.9 percent). This rise was translated into a real hourly wage increase of 6.5 percent.

As noted above, the gap between productivity and wages has resulted from some combination of erosions of worker bargaining power; increased international competition is a major reason why rates of return on capital have increased, returning to postwar highs. In Canada, corporate profits as a share of national income have increased from a recent low of 5.1 percent in 1991 and 1992 to 8.2 percent in 1995 and 1996 (third quarter). In the recent recovery (from 1992 to the third quarter of 1996), total wages and salaries in the business sector have increased by 16 percent, while pre-tax corporate profits have increased by 88 percent (Statistics Canada 1996c, p.89).

As a share of national income, corporate profits have still not returned to the 10 percent level of the 1980s or to the 11 percent to 12 percent levels of the 1950s and 1960s. One reason is the increased share of capital consumption allowances and indirect taxes in national income in the 1990s. The most important reason is that economywide corporate profits disguise a major gap between very low profitability in much of the domestic economy (e.g., retail trade, construction) and high profitability in export-oriented manufacturing, resources, and some parts of the service sector (particularly finance). While profit rates vary in general, they are at or near the peak levels of the 1980s in auto, electrical machinery and equipment, pulp and paper, and similar export sectors where large firms dominate. Statistics Canada (1996b, p. 3) recently reported that rates of return for large firms have recovered to the peak levels of the 1980s expansion.

From a labor perspective, the gap between productivity and wages is a cause of serious concern. Workers deserve to benefit from high and rising productivity—much of it achieved through work intensification—through higher living standards and shorter hours. The transmission belt from productivity to wages is also fundamentally important in macroeconomic terms. New technology will tend to be labor displacing unless the productivity gains to which it gives rise feed through into effective demand in the market. Shared benefits from higher productivity, as opposed to one-sided appropriation of those gains by capital, would also result in a much more equal society.

The policy implications of this analysis can be briefly summarized. We used to live in a world in which we had high productivity growth, which was shared by workers primarily through wage bargaining in relatively discrete national contexts. Today, we live in a world in which international competitiveness, high levels of unemployment and underemployment, and attacks on unions and labor standards have tipped the scales sharply in favor of capital. Balance needs to be restored, either through attenuation of the forces of international competitiveness, or through concerted international action to raise labor standards and the bargaining power of workers.

Endnotes

[1] As a technical aside, what is examined here is the difference between real wage growth and real production growth per unit of labor, with wages deflated by the CPI and production held down by the GDP deflator. Over the past decade, the CPI has increased by about 0.5 percent per year more than the GDP deflator, so figure 5.1 explains part of the gap. The difference between the two price measures lies in tax-driven increases in consumer prices and in the falling prices of capital equipment. The source of the data underlying the charts is *Statistics Canada* (1996c, p. 90) as reported in the Department of Finance Reference Tables 40.1 and 43. The wage measure—labor compensation per person hour—encompasses supplementary labor income, including payroll taxes paid by employers.

Bibliography

Bureau of Labor Statistics News. *International Comparisons of Manufacturing Productivity and Unit Labor Cost Trends, 1995.* USDL:96–284. Washington, D.C.: Author, July 17, 1996.

Industry Canada. "Strategies" Database. Ottawa: Author, 1996.

International Monetary Fund. *World Economic Outlook: A Survey by the Staff of the International Monetary Fund.* Washington, D.C.: Author, October 1995. ISBN 1-55775-467, stock # WEOEA.

Statistics Canada. *Annual Estimates of Employment, Earnings, and Hours.* Ottawa: Author, 1996a.

———. *The Daily.* 30 October 1966b. p. 3. Catalogue 11-001E. ISSN 0827-0485.

———. *System of National Accounts: Aggregate Productivity Measures.* Ottawa: Author, April 4, 1996c . Catalogue No. 15-204-XPE (paper). ISSN 0317-7882.

CHAPTER 6

Labor Market Developments, Trade, and Trade Agreements

Alan B. Krueger
Princeton University

I arrived at the Labor Department shortly after the North American Free Trade Agreement (NAFTA) had been ratified by the U.S. Congress. My predecessor as Chief Economist, Lawrence Katz, was assigned the job of negotiating the labor side agreements on behalf of the United States. I have always viewed that assignment as a once-in-a-lifetime opportunity for a labor economist. Few government policies are so universally well liked by economists as free trade agreements (although, as we shall see, the public is much more ambivalent about free trade). I arrived in time for the presidential administration's effort to increase the minimum wage, which, unlike free trade, was disliked by many economists but was widely supported by the public. In any event, I had the opportunity to observe the implementation of NAFTA, the side agreements, and the trade adjustment assistance.

In this article, I will discuss the profound changes that have taken place in the U.S. labor market over the past 15 years. Specifically, I will summarize recent trends in wages and employment at an aggregate and disaggregate level, explore reasons for those trends, and then probe the implications of labor market developments for trade agreements like NAFTA as I review public opinion polls concerning free trade agreements.

Trends in Aggregate Wages and Employment

The U.S. statistical agencies provide many different wage series for analysts to consider. Figure 6.1 displays five of the leading indicators of wage or compensation (wage and salary plus benefits), which have been indexed so their value in 1987 equals 100. These series differ for several reasons: some reflect different groups of workers (production and nonsupervisory versus all full-time workers); some report different summary statistics (mean versus median); some include fringe benefits, while others do not; and some report compensation per hour worked, while others report the average worker's hourly compensation. These legitimate and often subtle reasons are why the various series show somewhat different trends. However, my sense from studying the wage data is that they often differ by a wider margin than would be expected from these differences alone. For example, one would expect the Office of Productivity and Technology (OPT) within the Bureau of Labor Statistics (BLS) to have a compensation-per-hour measure that closely mirrors trends in the BLS's hourly compensation measure, which is derived from the Employment Cost Index (ECI) (measured in levels). However, these series have diverged by 6 percentage points since the ECI data were first produced with current weights in 1987. This gap is of great significance because the OPT series is most commonly used to compare wage and productivity growth; one gets a very different impression by using the other measures.

Despite these anomalies, several observations can be made regarding wage growth:

- These wage series have shown only modest or negative real growth in the past 15 years. Only the OPT compensation-per-hour measure shows positive real wage growth over this period.

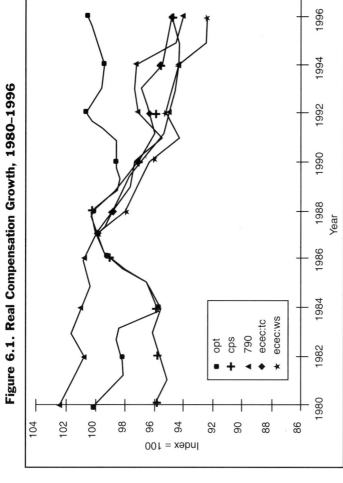

Figure 6.1. Real Compensation Growth, 1980–1996

Note: The abbreviation opt is the hourlu compensation shown by BLS's Office of Productivity and Technology; cps is the median weekly wage from Current Population Survey, 790 is the hourly wage of production/nonsupervisory workers from Current Establishment Survey, ecec:tc is the average hourly compensation cost in levels from the ECI survey, and ecec:ws is the hourly wage and salary in levels from the ECI survey.

113

- The "true" level of real wage growth depends critically on the price deflator one uses. I have a penchant for using the official BLS Cost Price Index—For All Urban Consumers (CPI-U) deflator, but a debate has raged in the United States over potential biases in the CPI. Unfortunately, much of this debate has taken place in the halls of Congress under the shadow of potential budgetary savings, rather than in the halls of academia. Nonetheless, there are real reasons to be concerned that the CPI may overstate inflation. It has been known for decades that a fixed-weight Laspeyres index like the CPI overstates the cost of living under certain conditions. Even more important, some aspects of the quality of products are difficult to measure and may lead the CPI to overstate the cost of living. Unfortunately, the extent of such a bias is impossible to estimate for the broad swatch of goods and services consumed in the United States, and any estimate available at present must rely on guesswork and subjective judgment. But it should be emphasized that whatever bias exists in the CPI today has probably existed at about the same order of magnitude in the past, so the slowdown in wage growth displayed in figure 6.1 is unlikely to be affected by this issue.

- Because these wage series show different trends, a comparison of wage and productivity growth naturally depends on which wage series is selected for such a comparison. The latest *Economic Report of the President* presents a graph of productivity growth and the OPT's compensation-per-hour measure in the post–World War II period. When hourly compensation is deflated by the CPI and productivity growth is deflated by the GDP deflator, a gap opens between these two series. However, the report points out that if the compensation series is deflated by the GDP deflator, the gap disappears; the two series have moved in tandem. The difference arises because the price of what we consume has grown more quickly than the price of what we produce, in large part because the price of investment goods (especially computers) has grown slowly. But, as noted above, the OPT compensation measure has grown more quickly than other compensation series, so other measures of compensation would still show a productivity-wage gap opening—even after accounting for the deflator differences.

- Another issue concerns recent wage growth. Several analysts have predicted that wage growth is currently rebounding from its downward trend, or is about to rebound. I have heard these predictions for at least 3 years. We are told that workers are about to lose their fear of job loss and gain the backbone needed to press for healthy wage gains. Personally, I find it difficult to see signs of an upturn in the recent wage data. The ECI, for example, continues to grow roughly at the pace of inflation, increasing by just 2.9 percent in the latest 12-month period. Some have viewed the fact that the wage component of the ECI has grown more sharply (3.3 percent) than the overall index (which also includes nonwage compensation)—a break from past trends—as a sign that compensation will pick up shortly. I am less sanguine about the prospects for rapid compensation growth in the near future. The recent slowdown in fringe benefit growth is mainly due to slower growth in employer health care expenditures. The slowdown in health care expenditures, in turn, is mainly due to a slowdown in overall insurance premium growth and a steady decline in the fraction of workers who receive employer-provided health insurance. I see few reasons for these trends to immediately reverse themselves (Krueger and Levy 1997). Moreover, I suspect that the same forces that have kept a lid on wage pressure are keeping a lid on fringe benefits.

- The reason for the slowdown in compensation growth that began in the 1970s is undoubtedly linked to the slowdown in productivity growth in the United States. A country can pay out in wages and profits only what it produces. Productivity growth determines the total output to be distributed. Of course, the distribution of output could change over time, but productivity growth determines that size of the total pie to be distributed, and productivity growth slowed down in the mid-1970s.

- Unlike wage growth, employment growth in the United States has been quite strong. Indeed, looking over the post–World War II period, the number of new jobs added each year has risen by almost a constant amount, fueled in large part by the entry of the baby boom cohort and women into the labor force. Figure 6.2 shows that most of Canada and the OECD Europe have experienced declines in the fraction of their adult populations who are working while the U.S. employment-to-population rate has continued to set new records.

Figure 6.2. Percentage of Adult Population Working, by Selected Countries

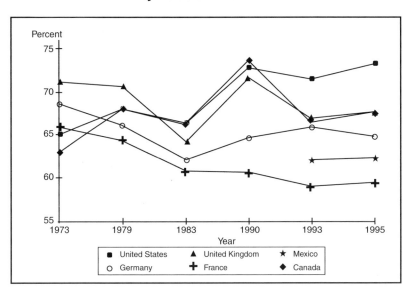

Source: OECD, *Employment Outlook*, Paris, 1996.

Disaggregated Trends

It must be stressed that the aggregate trends mask major differences in wage and employment trends across skill groups. For example, the real wage of the average male worker with a high school degree has fallen by more than 20 percent in the past 15 years, a much greater decline than was experienced by the median worker. Figure 6.3 shows the ratio of earnings of the median college graduate worker to the median high school graduate each year since 1980. The so-called payoff to education has reached record levels in the late 1980s and early 1990s. Other breakdowns by skill level (e.g., based on occupational categories) also show that skilled workers have experienced an increase in earnings, while less-skilled workers have suffered real declines in the past 15 years or so.

Figure 6.3. Payoff to Education Grows

(ratio of wages of college to high school graduates)

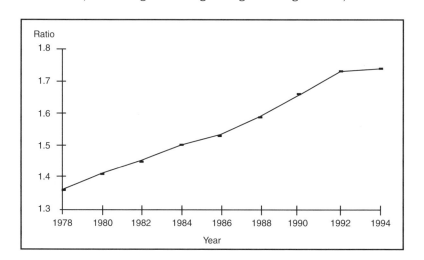

Meanwhile, the employment trends have been less favorable for less-skilled workers. For example, job growth has been much stronger in occupations that typically require higher education. Between 1984 and 1994, the fraction of the adult population that was employed fell by 10 percent for high school dropouts and by 3 percent for high school graduates, while it grew by 1 percent for college graduates. Figure 6.4 shows that the share of total hours contributed by college graduates increased from 20 percent in 1980 to 26 percent in 1994. Over the same time period, the college–high school wage ratio nearly doubled, from 40 to 78 percent.

Figure 6.4. Relative Hours and Pay Are Up for College Graduates, 1980–1994

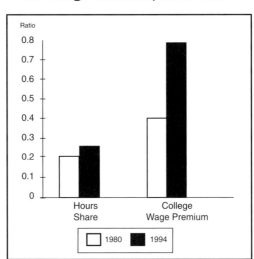

These wage and hour trends have profound implications for the distribution of income. Figure 6.5, for example, illustrates real family income growth by quintile of the income distribution between 1979 and 1993. The bottom of the income distribution suffered serious losses in income in the 1980s and early 1990s.

Figure 6.5. Real Family Income Growth by Quintile, 1979–1993

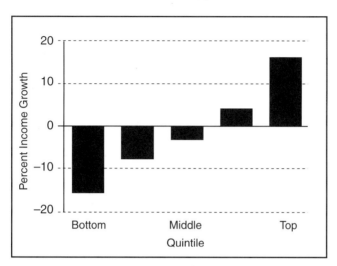

Source: U.S. Census Bureau. Current Population Survey. Annual Demographic Survey. Selected Characteristics of Households and Families by Quintile, March 1996.

Demand Shift

In the simplest supply-demand framework, the coincidence of rising quantities and rising prices documented above can be explained only by a shift of the demand curve; in this case, an increase in the demand for skilled workers relative to unskilled workers is illustrated in figure 6.6. Those of you who are familiar with my research will know that I do not think that the simple supply-demand framework can explain every phenomenon in the labor market. But in this situation, I think the simple supply-demand model has a lot to offer.

What might have caused the major shift in demand for skilled workers in the United States? There are two main explanations: (1) technological change that is "skill biased" and (2) expansion in trade with countries that are endowed with relatively many unskilled workers.

Figure 6.6. Demand for Skilled Workers Rises Relative to Unskilled Workers

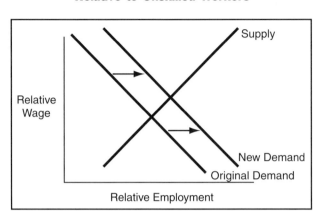

Computers

The most obvious form of technological change is the computer revolution, which is sweeping U.S. offices and factories. In 1983, only one-quarter of the workforce directly used a computer at work; by 1993, the figure climbed to almost half the workforce. Two types of evidence suggest that the spread of computers is a major cause of the demand shift for skilled workers.

First, workers who use computers on the job tend to be paid more than otherwise similar workers who do not use computers on the job (Krueger 1993). Of course, it is possible that the computer premium is merely reflecting unobserved characteristics of those who use computers, but the premium seems to exist even after controlling for a number of background factors, such as education and experience, and it exists in narrow occupations (such as secretaries). The expansion of computer use can account for one-third to two-thirds of the increase in the payoff to education between 1984 and 1993.

Second, the shift in employment toward more highly skilled workers has been greatest in the sectors that more intensively use computer technology (Autor, Katz, and Krueger 1997; and Berman, Bound, and Griliches 1994). Figure 6.7 shows that the share of workers with college degrees increased most between 1979 and 1993 in industries that had the greatest increase in computer use. David Autor, Larry Katz, and I estimate that the growth in computer technology can "explain" one-third to one-half of the increase in demand for skilled workers. We also find that the demand shift began in the 1970s, but was not immediately apparent because the supply of educated workers increased dramatically during the Vietnam War era and later in the 1970s.

Figure 6.7. Demand for Skilled Workers Rose Most in Industries with Greatest Expansion in Computers

(change in share of college graduates, 1979–1993)

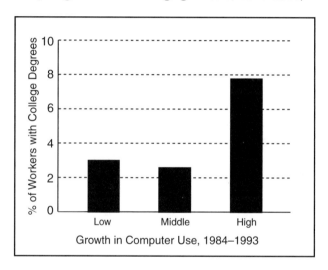

Trade

From the outset, I should make clear that I believe the heated rhetoric surrounding much of the debate over the impact of trade on wage inequality far outstrips the scientific precision with which we have been able to estimate the impact of trade on wages and employment. It is difficult to infer the effect of trade on wages and employment. Moreover, one would expect there to be interactions between the effects of trade and technology.

Theoretically, the effect of trade on wages is clear enough. If the United States expands trade with nations that are endowed with relatively more unskilled workers than is the United States, then the added competition should place downward pressure on the wage of unskilled workers in the United States and should lower the price of goods that use relatively many low-skilled workers in the production process. Nonetheless, freer trade creates winners and losers, and we expect that the gain to the winners exceeds the loss to the losers. (Of course, several caveats are needed for this story; see Bhagwati 1995.) Although the direction of the effect of trade on wages of unskilled workers can fairly confidently be predicted by economic theory, the magnitude of these effects is an empirical matter.

Essentially two types of evidence have been used to evaluate the role of trade.[1] The first, known as the "factor-content" model, calculates the amount of skilled and unskilled labor embodied in net imports to the United States. With the added assumption of the elasticity of demand for labor, the impact of this additional labor on low-skilled workers can be stimulated. The results of such calculations tend to suggest trade has played a relatively minor role in increasing wage inequality, around 10 percent or so (Borjas, Freeman, and Katz 1992; Sachs and Shatz 1994).

The factor-content approach has several shortcomings. First, the threat of trade may matter even if trade flows do not take place. For example, the fact that millions of Chinese workers are prepared to make cheap toys would put downward pressure on the price of domestically produced toys, and thereby on toymakers' wages, whether or not the Chinese workers actually produce the toys. Second, it is often unclear how to value the labor used in imports; it is unclear how much skilled and unskilled labor would be used to produce the products if they were produced domestically. Thus, the factor-content approach yields an answer, but it is unclear how much stock to place in the answer.

The second type of evidence, pioneered by Lawrence and Slaughter (1993), looks directly at prices. Trade should influence wages through its effect on prices. If an increase in trade with countries that are relatively endowed with low-skilled labor is the main source of the demand shift against unskilled workers in the United States, then one would expect product prices to be growing more slowly in sectors that intensively use less-skilled workers. If prices do not follow such a pattern, trade cannot be the explanation for the demand shift. The problem with this approach is that a number of other reasons—having nothing to do with trade—might account for an inverse relationship between product prices and skill intensity.

Lawrence and Slaughter (1993) find no relationship between import prices and skill intensity in a small sample of industries. Sachs and Shatz (1994), however, find a statistically significant, inverse relationship, as would be predicted if trade pressures caused the demand shift. Sachs and Shatz consider the relationship fairly weak; however, my own work suggests that the effect is not small, because labor's share in manufacturing industries is less than 20 percent (Krueger 1995). With unskilled labor's share so low, small price movements would require large wage adjustments to maintain constant profits.

My conclusion is that the magnitude of the price movements across sectors is *consistent* with trade being a major cause of the increase in relative demand for skilled workers. But it is also consistent with other explanations, such as some forms of technological change and deunionization. This type of evidence is much more useful if it can rule out trade as a suspect. Short of ruling out trade, however, it is unclear whether trade, technology, institutional changes, or other explanations have generated the inverse relationship between prices and skill intensity.

Whatever the role that trade has played in the past, I suspect that trade will place greater pressure on low-skilled workers in the future. The reason for this suspicion is simply that a great many unskilled workers in the world are paid very little. Figure 6.8, for example, documents the educational distribution of adults the world over by the year they left school. Around 1.5 billion potential workers leave school before they reached age 13; half the world's workers leave school at age 16 or earlier. When these workers are brought into global economic competition (because of greater openness, more political stability, and greater investment in developing countries), the consequences are unlikely to be positive for low-skilled workers in developed countries.

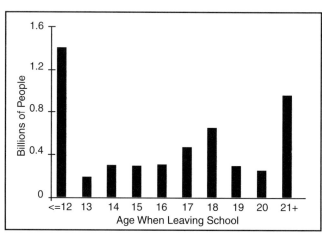

Figure 6.8. Distribution of Education, World Population Age 18–70 in 1990

Source: Author's calculations from World Values Surveys.

Economic and Public Opinion

Several surveys of the economics profession have been conducted to ascertain professional assessments of the various causes of rising inequality. These polls generally find a similar pattern: technology is cited as the main cause of rising inequality, with trade and institutional changes placing a distant second and third. Table 6.1 reports the results of one such poll. This particular poll reflects the views of about two dozen economists who attended a conference on wage inequality held by the New York Fed in 1995, and it illustrates how numbers can take on a life of their own. Unfortunately, I could not attend the New York Fed conference, so I asked my colleague Orley Ashenfelter to administer a short questionnaire to the attendees to summarize their views for me. Because for the most part I agreed with the results of the poll, I used it in a few presentations. Since then the numbers have appeared in the *New Yorker* magazine and in the 1997 *Economic Report of the President*, drawing more attention to the results than they probably deserve! Moreover, I now suspect that international trade is responsible for somewhat more than 10 percent of the changes that have taken place, and I feel somewhat guilty for treating the causes of in-equality as if they are mutually exclusive.

Table 6.1. Percentage of Rise in Wage Inequality Attributable to Different Sources

Sources	Average
New technologies	44.2%
Rising international trade	11.3
Decline in real value of minimum wage	9.1
Decline in unions	8.9
Rising immigration	6.6
Unknown factors	9.2
Other sources	10.9

Source: Survey of colloquium participants conducted at the New York Federal Reserve Board, Fall 1995.

In any event, the public views things quite different from the way the economics profession does. Blendon et al. (1997) conducted a survey of a random sample of adults, asking among other things, why the economy is not doing better than it is. The researchers asked the identical question to a random sample of 200 economists who were members of the American Economic Association and who reported having expertise on domestic matters. The differences between the two groups are striking. *Of the American public, 68 percent report that "companies are sending jobs overseas" is an important reason the economy is not doing better, while just 6 percent of economists agree with that statement.* Moreover, a higher percentage of non-college graduates (72 percent) cited jobs going overseas as a cause of the economy's problems than did college graduates (53 percent). This discrepancy probably reflects the differential wage and employment trends experienced by college and non-college graduates documented previously.

In view of the public's concern about jobs moving overseas, it is perhaps surprising that Blendon et al. (1997) find that a slim majority (55 percent) of the public believes that trade agreements between the United States and other countries are good for the economy. However, a much greater percentage (89 percent) of economists believe trade agreements are good for the U.S. economy.

Next consider the public's views specifically concerning NAFTA. Several polls have sought to ascertain the public's views about NAFTA. Because the responses to these questions are somewhat sensitive to the exact wording of the questions, it is important to compare similarly worded questions over time. Table 6.2 reports survey results of identically worded questions conducted by two separate polling organizations around the time NAFTA was passed and in October 1996. The results suggest that the public was roughly evenly divided in support of and in opposition to NAFTA around the time it passed. Since NAFTA has passed, the main trend has been an increase in the fraction of the public that reports not having enough information to form a view as to whether most people favor or oppose NAFTA. Two years after NAFTA took effect, fully 55 percent of the public did not have a view regarding it! I have reviewed several other polls, and they suggest a similar conclusion: the fraction of the public willing to venture a view about NAFTA has declined in the period since the trade agreement took effect.

Table 6.2. Opinion Poll—NAFTA

Do you favor or oppose the NAFTA with Mexico and Canada that eliminates nearly all restrictions on imports, exports, and business investment between Canada, Mexico, and the United States?			
	Associated Press 10/96	NBC/ Wall Street Journal 7/93	NBC/ Wall Street Journal 1/93
Favor	20%	31%	28%
Oppose	25	29	31
Have not heard enough/Don't know	55	40	41

On the whole, I think the public is fairly fickle about NAFTA. For example, in March 1996 the Yankelovich polling organization found that 51 percent of the American public opposed having the United States withdraw from NAFTA, whereas 34 percent of the public favored withdrawing from NAFTA (see table 6.3). Moreover, the fact that responses are sensitive to the wording of the questions also suggests that many people have not formed concrete views concerning their support of or opposition to NAFTA. Additional evidence of this national ambivalence was that NAFTA did not remain on the front burner of political issues that mattered most when people decided how to vote in the 1994 Congressional election, according to the Mitofisky exit poll.

Table 6.3. Opinion Poll—Withdrawing from NAFTA

Do you favor or oppose withdrawing the United States from NAFTA, which reduces trade barriers between Canada, Mexico, and the United States?	
Favor	34%
Oppose	51
Have not heard enough/Don't know	15

Source: Yankelovich Partners Poll of national registered voters, March 1996.

Nonetheless, a number of polls indicate that the public clearly believes freer trade (as represented by NAFTA and GATT) has negative consequences for American workers. A particularly interesting poll is presented in table 6.4. While the public is more likely to report free trade agreements like NAFTA and GATT as mostly good rather than as mostly bad for American corporations, consumers, and Wall Street, those people are more likely to report trade agreements as mostly bad for workers. Evidently, the public draws a distinction between the typical worker and the typical consumer. Further evidence that the public thinks NAFTA has been bad for American workers is in table 6.5, which shows that the public believes NAFTA has caused job losses in the United States and job gains in Canada and, especially, Mexico. One wonders what the public would think about NAFTA had post-1993 job growth in the United States been closer to the Canadian experience, rather than the impressive job growth that the nation actually has experienced.

The public believes that our trading partners have gained more from NAFTA than the United States has. For example, table 6.6 indicates that by a 4 to 1 margin the public believes that Mexico has benefited more than the United States from NAFTA. Another poll by Lou Harris and Associates in April 1995 indicated that the public also believes

Table 6.4. Opinion Poll—Free Trade Agreements

Do you think free trade agreements like NAFTA and GATT are mostly good or mostly bad for each of the following?				
	Companies	Consumers	Workers	Wall Street
Mostly Good	58%	45%	31%	57%
Mostly Bad	23	35	51	15
Not Sure	19	20	18	28

Source: Yankelovich Partners Poll of adult population, February 1996.

Table 6.5. Opinion Poll—NAFTA's Effects on Job Availability

Do you think the trade agreement, known as NAFTA, makes more jobs or fewer jobs in …?			
	Mexico	Canada	United States
More jobs	56%	39%	21%
Fewer jobs	12	17	47
About same	1	4	3
Don't know	32	40	29

Source: ICR Survey Research poll conducted for Associated Press, October 1996.

Table 6.6. Opinion Poll—Benefits of NAFTA
to United States and Mexico

Which country do you think benefits more from NAFTA—the United States or Mexico, both countries benefit equally, or neither of the countries benefit from the free trade agreement?	
United States	12%
Mexico	49
Both	16
Neither	9
Not sure	14

Source: Los Angeles Times poll of 1,572 adults nationwide, August 1996.

Canada and Mexico have benefited more from NAFTA than the United States has.

Finally, the scant evidence that is available suggests that the public supports labor and environmental side agreements such as those that were negotiated as part of NAFTA. For example, a poll conducted by Wirthlin Worldwide for BankBoston found that 73 percent of the U.S. public believes that labor and environmental standards should be negotiated as part of trade agreements, while 21 percent believes those issues should be treated separate from trade agreements (reported in PR Newswire, 1996).

Conclusion

Although it is common for economists to belittle the public's views about economic matters, I should stress that the public's views may be more relevant than the economists' in some instances. For example, if the public truly believes that jobs going overseas is a major threat, then job insecurity may be high and wage demands low as a consequence, whether that threat is real or illusory. Just as important, public opinion concerning trade agreements is likely to exert an important influence over the prospects for future trade agreements, so the public's view must be recognized. Moreover, given the uncertainty surrounding the existing academic literature on the impact of globalization on the U.S. workforce, I think the public's views should not be lightly dismissed in this case. Trade may be a major cause of the shift in demand against less-skilled workers, even if it is not the most important cause.

In view of the disappointing wage trends of the past 15 years, I frankly had expected the public opinion polls to turn up more evidence of widespread, visceral opposition to NAFTA and other trade agreements. The public as a whole, however, is probably best described as ambivalent to freer trade. Of course, a vocal minority may be strongly opposed to NAFTA and similar agreements, but this description does not fit the majority of the public. After all, that minority—the public and organizations strongly opposed to NAFTA—was unable to prevent it from passing. It is possible, however, that the public's ambivalence toward freer trade may turn to more strident opposition if the trend toward increasing wage disparity that has marked the past 15 years continues in the future. In addition to any other effects that they might have, labor and environmental side agreements may be a useful device for convincing the public to go along with trade agreements.

Endnotes

[1] Freeman (1995) provides an accessible treatment of these issues.

Bibliography

Autor, David; Lawrence Katz; and Alan Krueger. "Computing Inequality: Have Computers Changed the Labor Market?" Cambridge, Mass., National Bureau of Economic Research, 1997.

Berman, Eli; John Bound; and Zvi Griliches. "Changes in the Demand for Skilled Labor within U.S. Manufacturing Industries: Evidence from the Annual Survey of Manufacturing." *Quarterly Journal of Economics* (May 1994): 367–97.

Bhagwati, Jagdish. "Trade and Wages: Alternative Theoretical Approaches." Unpublished paper. New York: Columbia University, 1995.

Blendon, Robert; John Benson; Mollyann Brodie; Richard Morin; Drew Altman; Daniel Gitterman; Mario Brossard; and Matt James. "Bridging the Gap Between Public and Economists' Views of the Economy." *Journal of Economic Perspectives* (forthcoming 1997).

Borjas, George; Richard Freeman; and Lawrence Katz. "On the Labor Market Effects of Immigration and Trade." In *Immigration and the Work Force: Economic Consequences for the United States and Source Areas*, edited by G. Borjas and R. Freeman. Chicago: University of Chicago Press, 1992.

Freeman, Richard. "Are Your Wages Set in Beijing?" *The Journal of Economic Perspectives* 9, no. 3 (Summer 1995): 15–32.

Krueger, Alan. "How Computers Have Changed the Wage Structure: Evidence from Microdata, 1984–1989," *Quarterly Journal of Economics* 108, no. 1 (February 1993): 33–61.

———. "Labor Market Shifts and the Price Puzzle Revisited." Unpublished paper. Princeton, N.J.: Princeton University, 1995.

Krueger, Alan, and Helen Levy. "Accounting for the Slowdown in Employer Health Care Costs." Working paper. Cambridge, Mass: National Bureau of Economic Research, 1997.

Lawrence, Robert Z., and Matthew J. Slaughter. "Trade and U.S. Wages in the 1980's: Giant Sucking Sound or Small Hiccup." In *Brookings Papers on Economic Activity, Microeconomics* Vol. 2, 161–226. Washington, D.C.: Brookings Institute, 1993.

OECD. *Employment Outlook*. Paris: Organization for Economic Cooperation and Development, 1996.

Sachs, Jeffrey D., and Howard J. Shatz. "Trade and Jobs in U.S. Manufacturing." In *Brookings Papers on Economic Activity, Macroeconomics* Vol. 1, 1–84. Washington, D.C.: Brookings Institute, 1994.

U.S. Census Bureau. "Selected Characteristics of Households and Families by Quintile, March 1996." *Current Population Survey. Annual Demographic Survey*. Washington, D.C.: GPO, 1996.

CHAPTER 7

Changing Employment Relationships in the Open Economy: A Microeconomic Perspective

Ray Marshall
University of Texas at Austin

The Context

A more open economy, produced by the interactions of technology and the globalization of markets, has very important implications for employment relationships at the firm, or microeconomic, level. This is so because a more open system changes the context within which firms operate. The more traditional contexts usually stressed stability along with national, social, and political policies and were less concerned with competitive markets. For example, many national industries that have operated as oligopolies or as government-owned or -controlled monopolies are no longer tenable in a more competitive global economy where enterprises must justify themselves more in terms of the market and less on the basis of national, social, or political objectives. Similarly, national regulations to achieve stability have tended to protect workers or companies from the full impact of competitive market forces. And collective bargaining and regulatory processes to "take labor compensation out of competition" are more difficult to sustain in a more open economy.

The Competitiveness Challenge

A more open and knowledge-intensive economy requires firms, individuals, and governments to develop competitive strategies because the basic requirements of economic success in such an economy are different from those in more national, less-competitive systems. Traditional national economies give greater emphasis to physical resources; to social and political objectives for economic organizations; to stability through law, regulations, and contract; and to policies to control national economies. A more open and knowledge-intensive economy requires much greater attention to quality, productivity in the use of all resources, flexibility, international economies of scale, and development of human capital.

In a more open economy, productivity becomes more important in each producing unit because competition is achieved mainly by producing quality outputs at competitive costs. Only two ways exist to reduce costs: (1) directly through reducing prices or incomes and (2) indirectly through improving productivity, or output per unit of input. Quality—best defined as meeting customers' needs—becomes more important because open systems are more consumer driven; traditional, less-competitive systems are more producer driven. Flexibility becomes more important because a premium attaches to speed when meeting customers' needs and when responding to changing market and technological conditions.

Under competitive conditions, value added (i.e., productivity plus quality) is the only way to maintain and improve incomes. In the long run, a direct cost-cutting strategy implies (1) that a firm will either liquidate or shift production to low-wage places and (2) that, in high-wage countries, incomes for most workers will decline to international levels. In high-wage countries, the direct cost-cutting strategy also implies that in the long run incomes will become more unequal. Competition will drive wages to international levels for most workers, so that only those with scarce skills and knowledge will have relatively high incomes.

The microeconomic implication of these realities is that firms wishing to be viable in a particular country in the long run must stress flexibility and value added by all factors of production.

The traditional organization of mass production enterprises appeared to be highly productive because they achieved economies of scale from large aggregations of labor and fixed capital. However, these organizations had much waste and inflexibility that were offset by those economies of scale. In a more open, knowledge-intensive economy, technology makes it possible to reduce waste and become more flexible, as well as to achieve many of the benefits of scale without having that large scale.

The challenge of a strategy of high value-added competitiveness is to organize work to maximize or optimize both value added and flexibility. International evidence provides some insight into the nature of the high-performance systems required to achieve these objectives. Such systems include the following:

1. Lean, decentralized, participative management or governance systems. Lean means eliminating layers of management and decentralizing work as much as possible to front-line workers, thus eliminating the need for many management and staff workers. Substantial evidence shows that more participative systems can improve productivity, quality, and flexibility.

2. Positive reward systems that are equitable but provide incentives for workers to improve value added. Traditional systems motivate more out of fear (negative rewards) or even have perverse rewards, as when workers lose their jobs if they improve productivity.

3. Systems that develop and adapt appropriate technology. There is no unique competitive advantage in standardized technologies available to all firms. Companies get economic rents from technologies not readily available to competitors. Technology—best defined as how things are done—is essentially ideas, skill, and knowledge. Technological innovation improves value added through the use of technology that is best suited to particular enterprises and circumstances.

4. Systems with highly skilled managers and front-line workers. High-performance systems stress continuous individual and collective learning, as well as thinking, communication, interpersonal, self-managerial, and learning skills either not required or actually discouraged for front-line workers in traditional systems of mass production. The essence of high-performance companies is that they are efficient learning systems.

5. Systems with independent stakeholders. High-performance systems appear to function best when all stakeholders have independent sources of power to represent their interests in collaborative processes. Independent power strengthens trust and encourages high performance by all participants. Power improves stakeholders' alternatives and comes from a variety of sources, including transferability of physical or human capital, independent organizations, and legal protections for the rights given to various stakeholders.

It should be noted that this characterization of high-performance systems is an ideal type that probably describes less than 10 percent of U.S. firms. The best example I know of is General Motors' Saturn operation.

Implications for Public Policy

The competitiveness strategies adopted by companies have important implications for public welfare. The direct cost-cutting option implies lower wages and employment problems for many workers, as well as growing inequality of wages and income, all of which threaten democratic institutions and social stability. The lean production systems developed as part of the Japanese model pay more attention to productivity and quality than do traditional command and control systems, but those lean systems provide workers little independent power and require less attention to educating and training front-line workers than do high-performance systems.

A problem for public policy is that the achievement of the high value-added option requires a strategy. In most situations, a pure market national strategy would encourage cost-cutting strategies. Interventions, therefore, would be required to encourage companies to pursue high value-added strategies. Such interventions include (1) policies to encourage fair and effective competition to improve the quality and reduce the costs of goods, services, and factors of production; (2) policies to balance production and consumption; (3) policies to encourage the development of science, technology, human resources, and infrastructure; (4) provisions for social safety nets and worker participation in enterprise decisions; and (5) legal protections for the right of workers to organize and bargain collectively.

Implications for International Economic Institutions and Policies

A high value-added strategy also has clear implications for international economic institutions and policies. First, there is little doubt that an open and expanding global economy has been, and can be, a major institution or mechanism to improve the standards of living of people everywhere. However, several realities must be considered in modernizing international institutions and policies:

1. Market forces alone will not guarantee sustainable economic systems. Markets must operate within a framework that meets the standards of good rules, namely rules that are fair, transparent, and enforceable.

2. International institutions and policies should provide an equitable sharing of the benefits and costs of change. Market forces alone will cause a disproportionate share of the benefits to go to the strong and will shift a disproportionate share of the costs to the weak. It is particularly important to have effective policies that will help those who lose the most from international competition as they adjust to more competitive economic activities. Since international economic policies tend to be dominated by narrow commercial interests, there is a need for elected officials to protect broader interests. For example, many who favor free trade will resist policies to effectively adjust the labor market, despite their contentions that free trade produces huge benefits and that jobs are protected from international competition at great cost. An argument for embedding international economic policy in broader economic and social policies is to make those tradeoffs more explicit and transparent.

3. Policies and institutions should ensure that transactions are mutually beneficial between countries, as stipulated by the theory of comparative advantage. This theory assumes transactions to be almost entirely in final goods and services and to be of a purely voluntary

nature where competitive markets reveal comparative advantage. However, as international transactions become more important and extend to industries and capital flows, as well as to final products, there clearly can be winners and losers. The transactions might be "voluntary," but they are no longer restricted to decisions about whether to buy or sell final products. Instead, they concern whether to shift resources into low-wage places or to liquidate. Moreover, the competitiveness strategies developed have important implications for communities, nations, and workers, not just for companies.

4. A general principle for international policies and institutions should be to seek convergence of wages and working conditions more by raising low standards than by reducing higher ones. In other words, policies and institutions would be more viable if they were based on measures to encourage all countries to adopt high value-added strategies and minimize direct cost-cutting measures, especially where the latter involves suppressing wages and working conditions. There is an important difference between having low wages because of early stages of development and suppressing standards to gain a competitive advantage.

5. Labor standards like those outlined by the North American Agreement for Labor Cooperation (NAALC) can play a limited, but important, role in ensuring that international economic policies are mutually beneficial. The most important policies are those that increase the value added. However, there is no guarantee that workers' compensation will reflect productivity improvements. And labor standards are important for equity as well as for efficiency reasons: equity ensures that the weakest workers, companies, or countries do not bear a disproportionate share of the costs of change; and efficiency both internalizes social costs to enterprises that have the greatest power to deal with those costs efficiently, and tilts managerial decisions toward improving productivity instead of suppressing labor standards.

Conclusions

Here are answers to some specific questions raised by the speakers at the North American Seminar on Income and Productivity:

1. If there is declining economic security in North America, workers must rely less on employers and more on their own skills and resources, as well as on whatever social safety nets and public goods governments or other institutions can provide.

2. Constantly improving productivity implies a movement toward high-performance work places with positive reward systems.

3. New, more participative relationships are emerging that could help improve income and productivity.

The work of the NAALC's Commission for Labor Cooperation is important to all of our countries. The Commission's processes can help build consensus for sounder, mutually beneficial policies. Consensus begins with agreeing about the facts, concentrating on common interests, avoiding blame, and building trust. It seems to me that the Commission's processes could do all of those things.

CHAPTER 8

The Challenge of Workplace Innovation in Canada

Gordon Betcherman
Canadian Policy Research Networks and Ekos Research Associates

Canadians, like the citizens of so many other countries, are anxious about their jobs and their ability to cope with the pressures of a rapidly changing society. To some degree, this anxiety reflects a relatively weak labor market that is characterized by stubbornly high unemployment, stagnating wages, and polarization. However, it also reflects a deeper concern that stems from the erosion of traditional social and labor market institutions involving the employment contract, the labor-management relationship, the workplace practices, and the government policies.

For at least two generations, these traditional institutions—on the basis of long-term employment relationships, collective representation, labor regulations, and the public safety net—supported economic security and equity objectives. In doing so, they also enhanced economic efficiency. However, as the cumulative experience of the post-1975 period has shown, these post–World War II institutions (at least in their traditional form) are not well suited to the emerging techno-economic paradigm of the globally integrated, high-technology economy. Industrial-era employment contracts, as well as long-standing collective bargaining and workplace practices, have been judged as substandard from a competitiveness and innovation perspective and, at the same time, have become less effective in meeting the needs of workers. The post–World War II government programs have been threatened by fiscal problems and political disaffection.

As the traditional "anchors" have become less effective, we have not easily invented new ones to replace them. There is no doubt that we are in the midst of searching for practices, policies, and institutions that "fit" with the new techno-economic paradigm, and the Commission for Labor Cooperation is a good example. But we are still at a stage where technology and markets have surged ahead of our collective ability to cope with them. The challenge facing Canada—and, indeed, the NAFTA region overall—is to modernize workplace practices and related public policies in ways that (1) contribute to productivity and income distribution and (2) provide anchors to support the cohesion and integration that are the foundation of all successful societies.

The Age of Economic Anxiety[1]

Poll after poll reveals the economic anxiety that Canadians are experiencing. This concern is not unique to Canada. In fact, plenty of evidence shows widespread public concern in almost all countries about the forces of economic change. Consider, for example, the general strikes in France, which have been described by some commentators as "the first strike against globalization." And, in the United States, how else can we interpret the anger over massive layoffs at AT&T and other profitable corporations, or the unexpected receptivity to Pat Buchanan's isolationist message in the early stages of the 1996 presidential campaign?

It now seems possible that the anxiety expressed in events like these could ultimately constitute a serious political problem. Indeed, at the World Economic Forum in Davos, Switzerland, where global capitalism's elite meet annually, economic anxiety has become a prominent theme. Commentators at recent forums have acknowledged that the scale of restructuring, the growing gap between winners and losers, and the insecurity that blankets workplaces everywhere could potentially lead to a backlash against the prevailing economic strategy, which is based on global integration and technological innovation.

Public opinion polls indicate that Canadians are most concerned about the prospect of being without work. Throughout this decade, unemployment has consistently topped the list of pressing public issues. And, unlike the 1980s when apprehension about jobs fluctuated according to labor market conditions, concern in the 1990s about employment has been almost impervious to the ebb and flow of the economy. According to a national poll carried out by Ekos Research Associates Inc. in April 1996, 44 percent of those working thought there was a good chance that they could lose their job in the next couple of years. As figure 8.1 indicates, this concern rose slightly over the 2-year period that Ekos has asked this question (despite the fact that the unemployment rate actually fell during the period).

It should be understood that the personal vulnerability expressed through surveys such as these will ultimately affect the health of the economy. Throughout the recovery, consumer confidence has remained relatively low and, as a consequence, so has consumer spending.

Individual concerns are being driven not just by apprehensions about the forces of economic change. They also reflect the fact that Canadians see the rules of the workplace changing, which I will turn to in a later section. They see the social safety net being dismantled at the same time. We have heard the message from government that the public debt situation severely constrains what the state can do in terms of income support. The message now is that the key is a self-sufficiency based on acquiring skills and enhancing one's employability. By and large, Canadians have accepted this responsibility as suggested by survey results that training and education are now viewed as the "touchstone" for the future. However, Canadians are concerned about whether society will provide the support needed to acquire such skills. At the same time that our governments are cutting back on unemployment insurance and welfare, education and training funding is also threatened.

In the final analysis, then, the anxiety that Canadians are feeling has both a personal and a collective dimension. As the market seems to

Figure 8.1. Job Insecurity (General Public)

("I think there's a good chance I could lose my job in the next couple of years.")

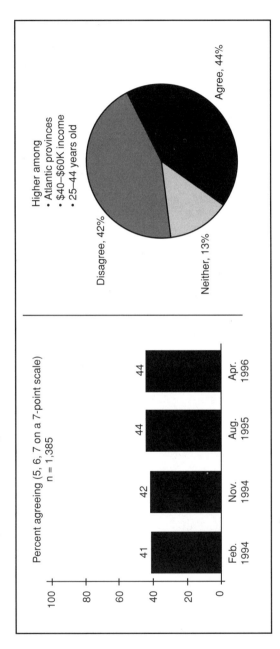

Percent agreeing (5, 6, 7 on a 7-point scale)
n = 1,385

Higher among
• Atlantic provinces
• $40–$60K income
• 25–44 years old

Agree, 44%

Neither, 13%

Disagree, 42%

Note: Reporduced with the permission of Ekos Research Associates Inc.
Source: Ekos Research Associates, Inc., "Rethinking Government 1995: Final Report" (unpublished).

provide less and less security, social spending is being cut, and people have less confidence that the anchors will be there to help them weather rough seas.

An Overview of Canadian Labor Market Trends

Before we turn to the issue of the workplace, a brief summary of the main labor market trends can help to situate the Canadian context. While many dimensions might be considered, I am going to touch on three that are prominent in the current debates in Canada: unemployment, earnings, and nonstandard jobs.

Persistently High Unemployment Rates

As we have seen, unemployment is the most pressing economic concern for Canadians. And, as figure 8.2 indicates, the long-term trend is not good. In the half-century since the end of World War II, unemployment rates have ratcheted up each decade. Here is a revealing statistic: before 1975, the average annual unemployment rate never got above 7.5 percent; since then it has not dropped below that level. During the 1990s, the unemployment rate has usually been in double digits, and even though we have technically been in a recovery for about 5 years now, it has not gone below 9 percent.[2]

The "structural" (as opposed to "cyclical") component of unemployment seems to have increased as well. So the problem is more complex than slow business or seasonal shutdowns. Increasingly, unemployment is driven by technological displacement, economic restructuring, or downsizing. This change has meant that all types of employees can be affected. It has also meant that long-term unemployment has become more prevalent.

Earnings Stagnation and Polarization

The average Canadian worker today earns little more in real terms than his or her counterpart did two decades ago. As figure 8.3 shows,

145

Figure 8.2. Unemployment Rate, 1946–1995

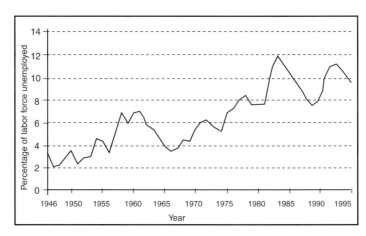

Source: Rachel Bernier, "The Labour Force Survey: 50 Years Old!" *The Labor Force*, November 1995. Statistics Canada, catalogue no. 71–001.

after three decades of robust wage gains, the growth in earnings slowed dramatically in the 1970s and essentially disappeared by the 1980s. This trend has continued during the 1990s, with mean (real) annual earnings less than $1,000 higher in 1995 than in 1990.[3]

Many explanations have been proposed for the earnings stagnation in Canada (just as in the United States). Some observers point to the increase in low-wage, nonstandard jobs that have accounted for much of the employment growth, particularly in the service sector. We will turn to this trend below. Others contend that the negotiating power of workers has declined in a cost-competitive business environment that is an unfavorable one for labor. It is true that, compared to the U.S. situation, Canadian unions have largely weathered the economic storms of the 1980s and 1990s. However, the unions have had to establish new bargaining priorities, mainly around job security, and wage negotiations have focused as much on avoiding freezes or rollbacks as on realizing new gains. While these and other factors have played some role, ultimately the flat earnings trend cannot be uncoupled from the productivity slowdown that we have experienced since the mid-1970s.

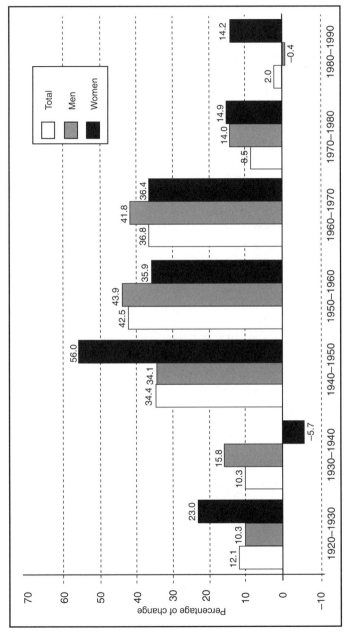

Figure 8.3. Percentage of Change in Average Wage Rates by Decade, 1920–1990

Legend:
- Total
- Men
- Women

1920–1930: Total 12.1, Men 10.3, Women 23.0
1930–1940: Total 10.3, Men 15.8, Women −5.7
1940–1950: Total 34.4, Men 34.1, Women 56.0
1950–1960: Total 42.5, Men 43.9, Women 35.9
1960–1970: Total 36.8, Men 41.8, Women 36.4
1970–1980: Total −8.5, Men 14.0, Women 14.9
1980–1990: Total 2.0, Men −0.4, Women 14.2

Percentage of change

Source: Abdul Rashid, "Seven Decades of Wage Changes." *Perspectives on Labour and Income*, 5, no. 2 (Summer 1993), p.13.

While distributional changes have not been as dramatic in Canada as in the United States, wages have become more polarized and unequal over the past two decades.[4] This change is particularly true for men and women working on a full-time, full-year basis.[5] Research indicates that the two principal factors underlying the changing distribution of earnings are a sharp decline in the relative wages of young workers and an increasingly unequal distribution of working time. Before taking up the work distribution question, it should be noted that the youth issue has assumed a high profile in Canada in recent years. Even with the modest improvement in aggregate labor market conditions since the 1990–1992 recession, the employment situation for young people has continued to deteriorate in many respects. In fact, the federal and provincial governments, while eschewing new active labor market initiatives, have, for the most part, placed a priority on developing programs for youth. That priority is in part because for many middle-aged baby boomers, an important source of economic anxiety is the difficulty their children are experiencing in establishing a foothold in the job market.

Nonstandard Jobs and the Redistribution of Work

The redistribution of working time is part of a broader trend away from the standard (full-time, continuous) employment arrangement that dominated during the postwar decades. Nonstandard work—especially part-time employment, but also short-term or temporary work, plus "own-account" self-employment—has increased steadily and now represents about one-third of all jobs (figure 8.4). It accounts for roughly half of the employment creation over the past two decades. Although some of this increase reflects employee preferences, much of it appears to be employer driven.[6] This fact is troubling because nonstandard jobs generally offer relatively low pay, few benefits, and little or no job security.

A retreat from the standard job is also evident in the polarization of working time. While the 35- to 40-hour work week is still the most typical arrangement, growing numbers of Canadians are working both shorter and longer hours. The part-time increase explains the growth

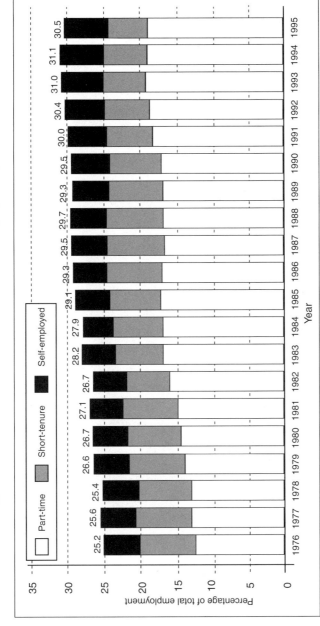

Figure 8.4. The Nonstandard Share of Total Employment, 1976–1995

Source: HRDC calculations are based on annual averages and unpublished data from Statistics Canada, Labour Force Survey. Persons in more than one type of nonstandard work are counted only once. Data for part-time employment use Statistics Canada's new definition of part-time, which includes individuals working two or more part-time jobs.

at the lower end, while increasing overtime accounts for the growth at the upper end. On the one hand, this latter development is of particular relevance, given the high levels of unemployment and underemployment and, on the other hand, the high degrees of time-stress (including work-and-family balancing problems) reported by many Canadians.

One final point on the work-time issue involves its link to the earnings polarization discussed above. In general, it is the more highly skilled (and paid) who are overrepresented in the group working long hours, and it is the less skilled in the short-time group. In part, this polarization seems to reflect skill bias of technological change. And, in part, it appears to be due to changes in the utilization and management of human resources in the Canadian workplace.

Changing Workplace Strategies[7]

A "micro," or organization-level, perspective is important to the present discussion on two counts. First, the rules in the workplace are changing, and, in many ways, these changes underlie the anxiety and uncertainty being experienced by workers. Second, many labor market and economic trends, including those summarized above, are being driven to some extent by changes in workplace strategies. In other words, there are key links between "macro" trends regarding unemployment, job creation, work and income distribution, and productivity growth, on the one hand, and "micro" policies and practices that play out at the level of the organization or workplace, on the other. This link pivots on knowledge generation and innovation that, in one direction, hold the keys to economic growth (and, thus, job creation) and, in the other direction, are themselves shaped to an important degree by organizational forces such as strategy, structure, and human resource and industrial relations practices.[8]

For several decades, the workplace strategies and practices of most Canadian organizations (like those in the United States) were based on centralization of decision making, on seniority-based labor deployment and compensation, on narrow job classifications, and on "job control" unionism. In terms of both internal and external relations, the logic was essentially to maximize stability and predictability. Starting in the early 1980s, however, the cumulative effect of deregulation, the liberalization of trade and investment, the productivity slowdown, and the computer revolution turned everything upside down. And, in response, the traditional systems began to be contested by employers as not being up to the emerging competitive challenges and of being too rigid in a business and technological environment that demanded flexibility above all.

Although a new dominant paradigm has not emerged, the traditional management systems have been irrevocably altered. For the most part, the changes in strategy and workplace practices have been initiated by employers to enhance enterprise flexibility. Innovations have been largely of two types (often occurring simultaneously). One has been directed toward increasing "numerical" flexibility, which refers to the ability of the firm to vary production inputs including labor, as required. Some methods have been hiring and laying off employees, altering hours of work, using part-time and contract workers, and subcontracting or outsourcing work. The other type of innovation has been to enhance "functional" flexibility through work reorganization that includes, for example, delayering; creating fluid job designs; multiskilling; and using self-managed, multifunctional teams.[9]

In the North American context, these organizational strategies have often taken forms that have become known as "core-periphery" and "lean production" models. In the former, employers rely primarily on a "core" of experienced, skilled employees that is augmented, as needed, by a pool of less-skilled and inexpensive "periphery" workers who are typically employed in nonstandard work forms. "Lean production" systems also rely on a core of skilled employees, with many components of the final product or service and with supporting activities provided by outside suppliers. Both of these models are meant to simultaneously increase functional and numerical flexibility—the former through high-performance workplace practices (with respect to job design, training, information-sharing, etc.) for core employees, and the latter through the use of either peripheral employees or outsourcing and subcontracting.

There is little need to elaborate on the importance of technological innovation in all of this, beyond underlining the point that new information and communication technologies, along with their potential for altering the work process, have spurred much of the workplace change. Generally, innovations such as those described above have been built around such technologies. Those innovations have replaced traditional strategies that are based on hierarchy, rigid task divisions, and fixed organizational boundaries that have become increasingly inappropriate with the diffusion of successive generations of flexible technologies.

Although the reshaping of the human resource management paradigm is far from complete, workplace innovation thus far (and the future that such innovation points to) has a number of implications for workers, for their unions, and for the labor market and society more broadly.[10]

To begin, the employment effects of workplace innovations—especially those designed to increase numerical flexibility—have reduced job security virtually by definition and, thus, have reduced longer-run economic security. This result has occurred through rationalization and downsizing, through outsourcing and subcontracting (which have led to the relative growth of self-employment and employment in micro firms), and through the growth of nonstandard work.

These effects, however, are not uniform. Organizational change has different implications for different people, and the net result has been to contribute to the polarization in the labor market. Many of the features of the high-performance workplace—for example, core-periphery systems and performance-based pay—contribute to the segmentation. Moreover, the patterns of human capital investment appear to be an exacerbating factor, with investment increasingly concentrated on core employees or other "knowledge" workers who are already well educated and highly skilled. In the final analysis, the transformation of work presents opportunities for some that can be translated into new skills, a better income, and upward mobility while, for others, the changes are leading to insecurity and marginalization.

New workplace strategies have raised a number of issues for unions, with uncertain implications for the future direction of collective representation. Despite the relative strength of the Canadian labor movement, there is no doubt that workplace change and economic restructuring, along with the attendant redirection of industrial relations, have created a number of serious pressure points for unions. The shifts in employment resulting from subcontracting and nonstandard work have raised new organizing and membership challenges. The management initiatives to increase functional flexibility and to lower costs have altered the bargaining agenda and have led to the erosion of long-standing protections. And while organizational change, in some cases, has offered unions new partnership opportunities, it has more often forced unions into a defensive mode.

Ultimately, the changing employment and industrial relations systems are leading to an individualization of risk and responsibility. The traditional work institutions provided stability, certainty, and a collective insurance against the disruptions of economic and technological change. As these institutions weaken, and as the social support provided by government diminishes, the onus is increasingly on individuals to make their own way in the new economy.

Looking to the Future

Concerns about the future of work are not new. However, there are periods when technological innovation and economic restructuring are particularly rapid and profound. Not only are these periods—shifts in the "techno-economic paradigm"—characterized by a great deal of economic turbulence, but also the anchors provided by existing social institutions become less effective in helping people adjust to the changing times.

This combination of a fundamental economic change and of a weakening institutional framework that is less capable of providing collective security is at the heart of the uncertainty that workers are feeling. The aggregate labor market difficulties described earlier do not, by themselves, account for everything. The weakening of collective institutions associated with the rules of the workplace, the employment contract, the collective representation, and the social safety net is also a key factor. The result is that, as these anchors have become less effective, the risks associated with economic and technological restructuring are increasingly borne by individual Canadians and their families. If this trend continues, we face the prospect of polarization and social fragmentation and an economy that is stunted by (1) an underutilization of its human resources, (2) a depressed consumer base, and (3) large numbers of people who will resist change even when it really does represent progress.

The challenge now is to invent new anchors, or modernize old ones, that can strengthen the capacity of individuals to adapt to change and that can provide more appropriate collective security. This obviously huge task encompasses a breadth of issues far beyond what this article might consider. However, given the focus of this session, it seems appropriate to return to the workplace arena and reflect on how we might create the environment and incentives that support the diffusion of best practice organizational models that both foster the innovation underlying strong firm performance and serve the interests of employees. The traditional post–World War II employment systems no longer meet these criteria, but neither does much of the workplace change that has occurred in recent years.

A number of barriers both constrain the diffusion of best practice innovation and limit the effectiveness of the innovation that does occur. The first type of obstacle concerns market failures (caused by information barriers and externalities), which lead to an underinvestment in human capital by many enterprises. A second relates to the divergent interests, at least in the short run, of employers and employees. This difference heightens a natural unwillingness to take the risks inherent in redefining roles, responsibilities, and relationships, a redefining that is necessary in changing workplace systems. Institutional frameworks and public policies often impede the diffusion and sustainability of organizational innovation. These impediments range from corporate governance and financial market institutions that emphasize shareholders' short-run interests (above longer-term interests or those of other stakeholders) to labor market regulations that create hiring or training disincentives.

Overcoming these barriers will require concerted efforts on the part of all stakeholders. Ultimately, though, the contours of the workplace will be defined by choices made by employers and employees. And while the perspectives of each do differ, the way forward lies with recognizing that those interests around the workplace do converge over the longer run, as the tradeoff between competitiveness and security becomes far less stark.

Governments, however, also have a part to play in supporting the diffusion of best practice organizational change. Since human capital investment is at the core of both the knowledge generation and the innovation that underlie such change, the clearest priorities are education and training. At a minimum, human resource development policy must provide basic-skills education; must support an efficient human capital market through information, counseling, and standard-setting; must promote linkages within the education sector and between that sector and the labor market; and must guarantee that selective access problems are confronted.

However, governments must go beyond education and training and should address a range of other concerns. In conclusion, I want to touch on two of the most critical issues: (1) supporting economic security and (2) helping to refashion the very nature of the postindustrial social contract.

I began with the observation that widespread economic insecurity appears to be entangled in the transition to the postindustrial economy. Certainly, the diffusion of more flexible organizational models is one source of that insecurity. Governments must place a high priority on how to provide security in the new environment. Admittedly, *security* is likely to be defined differently in the future than it was previously. More specifically, in the industrial paradigm of the post–World War II decades, the notion of security involved protection *from* change. Security is now being redefined in the emerging postindustrial paradigm as the ability *to* change. Thus, policy issues discussed above about human capital are absolutely central to the reconceptualization of how economic security will be provided.

Moreover, in the industrial era, security was closely linked to having a job. Not only has the income from work obviously been a key element in that security, but also social programs and benefits in most countries have been tied to the state of employment. However, if the various nonstandard work arrangements (self-employment, independent contracting, temporary work, etc.) that are now proliferating do, in fact, describe employment in the postindustrial economy, new strategies will have to be devised that can uncouple security from the job and can accommodate more varied patterns of activity. This concept applies to insurance and benefit programs, plus the framework for worker representation.

Indeed, a renewed concept of security will be an important cornerstone of the postindustrial social contract. A workable social contract—the explicit or implicit definition of how roles, responsibilities, and rewards are distributed across the society's stakeholders—is a necessary condition for a strong economy and a cohesive society. During the prosperous post–World War II decades, two cornerstones of the social contract in most industrialized countries were the goal of (1) full employment and (2) a welfare state that provided social security and collective insurance. However, as these cornerstones have weakened, the social contract they supported has become more fragile.

The implications of this change have been reflected in social relations at the workplace level. Where employers have introduced flexibility initiatives, the security of a quid pro quo has often not existed for labor. This insecurity, which is based on an absence of workplace-level guarantees, has been exacerbated by the erosion of societal supports in the form of full employment and protection offered by the welfare state. These conditions have dampened labor's enthusiasm for change; have likely slowed the diffusion of productivity-enhancing innovation in some cases; and have, more often, impeded the durability and effectiveness of the change that has occurred.

Thus, a revitalization of the social contract, along with its corresponding bargain at the workplace level, is necessary for sustainable innovation to occur. While the basis of a new consensus is not yet clear, a key will likely be access to education and training that, in turn, will foster lifelong learning and will enhance employability. However, opportunities for human capital investment alone will not be enough for a workable social contract without some notion of economic insurance that provides a collective pooling of risk. All of these changes pose formidable challenges for governments, both in terms of ensuring that the institutional framework provides incentives for the stakeholders to work toward a consensus and in terms of working with them to identify and articulate the cornerstones of that consensus.

Endnotes

[1] The next two sections are drawn from Betcherman and Lowe (1997).

[2] Official rates, of course, do not capture the full extent of "joblessness." Calculations that include discouraged workers and involuntary part-time workers, for example, lead to considerably higher estimates of unemployment.

[3] This figure pertains to full-year, full-time workers. In fact, there has been some gain among women during the 1990s, but this gain has been offset by a slight decline among men. See Statistics Canada, *The Daily*, 27 January 1997.

[4] It is also the case that the distribution of total income (i.e., earnings plus other sources of income) has been relatively stable. This stability is due to the equalizing role of the tax-and-transfer system. Thus, the prospects of a reduced redistributive role of government raise concerns for some about greater inequality in the distribution of total income.

[5] The earnings distribution for all women has not become more unequal, primarily because of earnings gains (through more hours worked) experienced by part-time and/or part-year working women. The earnings distribution trends are taken from Morissett, Myles, and Picot (1994).

[6] The one component of nonstandard employment where it is possible to gauge the relative importance of employee versus employer preferences is part-time work. The most recent statistics indicate that about one-third of part-time workers are "involuntary" (would prefer full-time work). In the mid-1970s, the involuntary share was about 10 percent.

[7] For an extended discussion of the issues addressed in this section and the next, see Betcherman (1997).

[8] For a discussion of these relationships, see OECD (1996), especially chapter 6.

[9] It is difficult to precisely measure the diffusion of nontraditional workplace models. National statistical agencies do not collect data on organizational practices. Indeed, these practices are not easily captured quantitatively. The OECD estimates that about one-quarter of all enterprises have adopted some form of flexible, organizational system. The incidence may be slightly higher in North America. In any case, the

research consistently shows that workplace innovation has been most widely diffused among large, technologically sophisticated enterprises, thus competing in industries exposed to international competition.

[10] The research, while often imprecise and far from unanimous, does conclude that flexible workplace innovations, especially high-performance practices, can have positive performance impacts for firms. This research suggests that these systems can be expected to diffuse further. For a summary of the (largely American) analysis linking human resource strategies with firm performance, see Ichniowski et al. (1996).

Bibliography

Bernier, Rachel. "The Labour Force Survey: 50 Years Old!" The Labour Force, catalogue no. 71–001. Ottawa: Statistics Canada, November 1995.

Betcherman, Gordon. *Changing Workplace Strategies: Achieving Better Outcomes.* Paris and Ottawa: OECD and Human Resources Development Canada, 1997.

Betcherman, Gordon, and Graham Lowe. *The Future of Work in Canada: A Synthesis Report.* Ottawa: Canadian Policy Research Networks, 1997.

Ekos Research Associates Inc. "National Poll." Ottawa: Author, April 1996.

Ekos Research Associates Inc. "Rethinking Government 1995: Final Report." Ottawa: Author. Forthcoming.

Ichniowski, Casey; Thomas A. Kochan; David Levine; Craig Olson; and George Strauss. "What Works at Work: Overview and Assessment." *Industrial Relations* 35, no. 3 (July 1996).

Morissett, René; John Myles; and Garnett Picot. "Earnings Inequality and the Distribution of Working Time in Canada." *Canadian Business Economics* 2, no. 3 (Spring 1994).

Organization for Economic Cooperation and Development. *Technology, Productivity, and Job Creation*. Paris: OECD, 1996).

Rashid, Abdul. "Seven Decades of Wage Changes." *Perspectives on Labour and Income* vol. 5, no. 2 (Summer 1993): 13.

Statistics Canada, *The Daily*, 27 January 1997.

CHAPTER 9

Technological Change, Trade Liberalization, and Change in the Business Climate in Mexico

Norma Samaniego-Breach
Universidad Iberoamericana and Santa Fe Consultores

The issue of productivity has only recently become a matter of interest in Mexico. From 1950 to 1970, the Mexican economy grew at an average of 7 percent, which is quite high by international standards. The development strategy chosen, which is very different from the one adopted in the Asian countries, was based on the model of a closed economy. This model consists of high foreign trade barriers and the substitution of imports that require simple technologies, which are under high tariff protection, along with a captive domestic market. Companies flourished in this climate. Since they faced no external competition and had an ensured demand, they did not place sufficient stress on quality or productivity.

Economic development strategy has changed radically in the past 15 years. The economy was shaken by severe crises that forced companies and the public sector to rethink their strategies and forms of organization. Over that period, the world also experienced sweeping changes. Globalization and the rapid spread of new technologies have toppled the walls of companies that had been built up since the Industrial

Revolution. New production opportunities are now erasing the borders of space and time. Thus, many traditional organizations worldwide, including companies, have had to undertake intensive restructuring programs or be left behind.

These developments and the heavy shocks to the Mexican economy since the 1950s, when the industrialization process began, have made the country increasingly sensitive to changes on the global level and have awakened an interest in productivity. This article describes the process and explains some of the trends that can be seen inside companies.

The Import Substitution Process and Its Limitations

When industrialization began in Mexico in the 1950s, a broad horizon existed for import substitution, and there was an ensured demand for the products. However, as progress was made toward import substitution, the possibilities of substituting simple technologies began to be exhausted and growth in production slowed. Sales of Mexican products abroad were limited to exports of raw materials—minerals and agricultural products—that were exposed to swings in international prices. The manufactured goods exported from time to time (mainly to sell surpluses) were often subsidized by high domestic prices.

The economy and industry reached the point where there was no spur for growth, precisely at a time when the labor supply had climbed to a historical peak. In this difficult situation, it was decided to preserve jobs and industrial growth through greater government intervention in the economy, which led to rising debt and the beginning of the inflation phenomenon. At the same time, the discovery of large fossil fuel reserves, plus the large investments channeled into that sector, turned oil into the main source of foreign currency and an attractive source for heavier borrowing. The strategy of stimulating growth by increasing debt failed in 1982 with the collapse of international oil prices, which was compounded by the economy's inability to honor the foreign debt commitments that had been contracted in the late 1970s and early 1980s.

The Crisis and the Change in Strategy

As a result of the 1982 crisis, the economy was subject to a harsh and protracted adjustment to balance the high fiscal deficit and to honor Mexico's foreign financial commitments. Public spending was cut back sharply, and the role of government in the economy was reduced. In 1986, a rapid process of trade liberalization was launched with Mexico's entry into the General Agreement on Tariffs and Trade (GATT), which was consolidated later with renegotiation of the North American Free Trade Agreement (NAFTA).

The crisis and the adjustments, together with structural change, led to a much slower rate of growth in the 1980s than in the two previous decades (1.8 percent a year as compared to 7 percent from 1950 to 1970).

Annual inflation, which had risen to a historical high in 1987 when it hit 160 percent, was brought down to 7 percent in 1994, when the economy began to grow again. However, the external deficit piled up during this period. This situation and the sudden collapse of the exchange rate as a nominal anchor led at the end of 1994 to a new and severe crisis, the worst in Mexico's recent history. In 1995, Gross Domestic Product (GDP) shrank by 6.2 percent in real terms, and employment in the modern sector suffered a sharp and widespread drop. Unlike 1982, during this crisis there has been a quicker recovery in economic growth, employment, and access to external capital markets. However, Mexico is still far from the real levels that applied before the crisis, and the country has experienced high underemployment.

Productivity During the Start-Up of the Industrialization Process

One serious limitation that can be attributed to the industrialization process in Mexico was the excessive stress on high growth rates and the scant attention to other variables such as productivity, employment, and distribution. Few studies take an in-depth look at productivity from 1950 to 1970 although, despite statistical limitations, some analysts had been warning of this serious structural problem since the 1960s. Using data from the 1960 input-product matrix, Boon (1968) observed (1) that productivity levels in the manufacturing sector, which he grouped into eight branches, were excessively low in comparison to international standards, and (2) that although wages were also low, they were high in comparison to domestic levels of productivity. He also noted that, in comparison with the United States and the United Kingdom, some branches such as steel and nonmetal mineral manufactures were even more inefficient, since they used more labor and more capital per unit of product.

Different studies conducted subsequently, including one by the World Bank (1986) and one by Enrique Hernández Laos (1973), coincide in noting that during the 1950s, 1960s, and 1970s, total factor productivity grew very modestly. One of the estimates (World Bank 1986) places it at 0.8 percent a year, while another (Boon 1968) gives a figure of 0.7 percent for 1970–1980, with negative rates in some branches of industry.

How, then, can the very high economic growth during the start-up of the industrialization process be explained? Some analysts have concluded that high economic growth with very low productivity levels and rates, such as those that prevailed during the industrialization stage in Mexico, can be explained only through a massive accretion of capital and labor, which was enormously costly for the country. Each additional unit of value added required more capital and labor than would have been necessary in other economies (not only in the more highly industrialized economies, but also in countries in a development stage similar to Mexico's).

A study conducted by Dollar and Sokoloff (1990) points to the differences that prevailed in the 1960s and 1970s between two economies—Mexico and South Korea—that followed different directions in their development processes. Both researchers conclude that while South Korea saw growth in factor productivity of almost 6 percent a year from 1963 to 1979, in Mexico total factor productivity from 1970 to 1981 rose by a scant 0.8 percent a year, contributing very little to growth in GDP.

At that time there was not the same interest in productivity in Mexico as there is today. Since the domestically manufactured products were the only ones available on the market, they were not threatened by competition from imports. The neglect of this aspect cost the country very dearly, leading it to depend on excessively high increases in capital (its scarcest factor) in order to boost production.

Trade Liberalization and Productivity

The crises at the start of the 1980s and in the following decade meant a period of severe growth contraction, stagnation, and retrenchment for Mexico. During that time, when the world was embarking on the adventure of free markets, when fresh breezes blew to thaw out conditions, and when new players appeared on the economic scene, Mexico could not have returned to its old closed market. That market had had its heyday, producing high growth rates as well as serious constraints on development, but the market had been based on high concentrations of economic activity and income. It was necessary for Mexico to return to the path of growth, but to find new avenues.

In the mid-1980s, the country started down the path to open trade in a rapid unilateral process of lowering tariffs. The rules of the game in this new context, which was uncharted territory for many individuals and companies, were based on a new idea, competitiveness, which would become the key to success or failure. The domestic market was suddenly flooded by a wide variety of foreign products, which consumers coveted after so many years of customs restrictions, quotas, and tariffs that had made those products inaccessible. Many products were of superior quality, but in some cases, consumers were attracted by their novelty.

What Happened to Mexican Productivity During the 1980s?

The most recent studies indicate that productivity in the 1980s had mixed components. Until 1984, this variable showed a new drop, linked to particularly inefficient use of installed capacity after the 1982 crisis. A large part of the production plant remained idle, although employment did not drop to the same degree as production. In the second half of the decade, signs of growth began to appear, but they started from very low levels of productivity, which applied throughout virtually all branches of the manufacturing sector (Hernández Laos 1994b).

How Can Mexican Productivity Growth Levels and Rates Be Assessed in Comparison with Other Countries?

Comparative studies between countries' productivity rates and trends are scarce and present serious drawbacks owing to the different nature of the statistical information used and differences in methodology. This field calls for more research, particularly if conducted jointly with specialists in the countries to be compared, if such comparisons are to ensure that the results are as useful as possible in different contexts.

One recent attempt at comparative analysis is a study by Hernández Laos (1994a), which analyzes the marked differences when comparing labor productivity in Mexico, to that in the United States and Canada from 1970 to 1988. He shows that at the start of the 1970s, GDP per worker in Mexico, valued in homogeneous purchasing power units, was 39 percent of the figure that applied in the United States and 43 percent of the Canadian figure. This gap appears to have narrowed slightly from 1970 to 1981, but it widened again between 1981 and 1988.

What Is Going On in Companies?

Studies of productivity in Mexico from 1987 to 1996 are still scarce and lack a broad enough historical perspective. In that period, the phenomenon is clouded by a number of structural changes and violent economic shocks. What has the real effect of trade liberalization been since Mexico entered GATT and later embarked on free trade with the United States and Canada? How does Mexico's productivity behave as a whole and by sector and branch of economic activity? What trends have appeared in the macroeconomic organization of production, in the establishment or breakdown of production chains, in human resource training and education policies, in wages, and in the introduction and dissemination of technologies?

One response is that over this period attitudes toward productivity have been changing significantly. Once a distant and theoretical term, productivity has become a real concern and a serious and imminent threat. Mexico's lack of past experience with open international competition in the production of domestic goods has forced entrepreneurs and workers into a new context in which many industries have had to learn harsh lessons from their long neglect of quality and productivity levels. Free trade has accelerated the process of structural transformation and natural selection of the fittest, and many small- and medium-sized companies have been literally swept away by competition, with their production replaced by goods from more developed countries or from competitors in Asia. Some industries, such as the toy industry, have almost disappeared, and the production chains have broken down among small and medium companies that supplied large industries.

The surviving production units have been forced to readjust their workforce levels, introduce new technologies, and take an outward-looking approach. New areas for development have arisen in export-oriented industries. Among company marketing strategies, exports have become more attractive in view of (1) a weak domestic demand that is in the wake of a long period of economic shrinkage, (2) a meager purchasing power, and (3) a simultaneous structural change in which the public sector has ceased to be the driving force of the economy.

Under these circumstances, the strategy for raising productivity is seen as a defensive measure in the face of rapid trade liberalization. It is also seen as a way of cutting back on excessive costs, rationalizing processes, and preventing the closure of plants and the loss of even more jobs. Companies that have not closed have instead begun to examine their practices and processes as they try to prevent waste and to trim their personnel and indirect costs. The different levels and sectors are taking a new approach to analyzing their management processes and to improving quality and productivity.

There is now greater acceptance of a more expeditious introduction of new technologies, quality certification, and better training and updating for the workforce. This trend does not apply across the board, however, since small and medium companies in sectors that are not as exposed to foreign competition, particularly small business and more traditional services, continue to lag behind. Polarization can also be seen in the manufacturing industry, where productive units (which have opened to trade abroad by using technologies and management practices that are more in tune with the advanced countries) coexist with other companies (which cling to survival under such difficult conditions that they cannot plan much beyond tomorrow).

What Impact Has the Change in Production Processes Had on Industry as a Whole and by Branch?

Although the issues of productivity and globalization have become hot topics in all business environments in Mexico, changes in organization to boost productivity have still not extended to the entire productive plant. A nationwide survey (STPS 1995) of the manufacturing sector from 1989 to 1992 indicates that just 14 percent of the companies had made major changes in how they organize their production.

In general, the changes began with the large- and medium-sized companies that were most directly involved in foreign trade. The study suggests that about two-thirds of those companies had begun some kind of restructuring between 1989 and 1992, while only 47.7 percent of small companies (with 15 to 100 employees) had done so. Signs of change in microenterprises were still minimal. By branch of activity, businesses oriented to the foreign market and those affected by competition were the first to reorganize, particularly the pharmaceuticals; the domestic appliance manufacture and assembly; and the steel, automotive, and paper industries.

The actions undertaken have differed significantly, depending on the size of the companies and their relative degree of modernization when trade liberalization began. The survey (STPS 1995) shows that one of the most frequent changes in all types of production units has been the introduction of new machinery and technology. However, in large companies, changes of this kind have gone hand-in-hand with greater attention to developing statistical indicators to control production processes. Such attention also includes adopting systems that will improve quality and productivity as reflected in strategies to reduce waste, produce fewer defective parts, reduce downtime, provide better service for clients, decrease accidents and work-related illnesses, and use stricter health control measures. Mid-sized companies have favored adopting new supervisory systems, and the most frequent practice introduced by microenterprises has been job rotation.

One clear trend that can be seen in several capital-intensive areas, such as the steel and automotive industries, has been reorganization to react more quickly to specific demand. In those cases, the idea is to transform rigid systems of mass production into more flexible systems that can respond better to changing needs and market tastes.

The survey (STPS 1995) reports that one-third of the companies that have gone furthest in this direction have increases in productivity. The production of another third of the companies is better adapted to client preferences and needs, and the quality levels of that third have improved. To a lesser extent, labor-management relations have improved, and workers are more involved in decision-making processes.

As in other countries, adjustments in Mexico have tended to demand higher levels of worker skills and greater accountability by employees involved directly in production. This particularly interesting result implies major changes in the short term among the profiles of manufacturing industry workers, along with a growing shift away from mass-production models that use unskilled labor.

When looked at by size, small companies are most in need of upgrading worker skills. Medium-sized and large companies have demanded relatively higher levels of training and specialization for some time now. Almost four-fifths of the companies that reorganized have increased the levels of accountability and independence of their employees. The exception is assembly plants, which still maintain vertical lines of authority and whose work teams have not been given as much responsibility as in other industries.

The decision-making areas in which employees participate most are health and safety, followed by quality committees, as well as task forces to increase productivity. In the five branches of industry that underwent the most sweeping reorganization, employee participation in company decisions is considerably higher than the national average (from 70 percent to 80 percent as compared to 50 percent).

The survey also shows that unionization has not been an obstacle to the reorganization of production. The branches that have undergone the greatest changes in their organizational systems are precisely those with the highest rates of unionization, particularly the pharmaceutical, steel, and automotive industries, where 60 percent of establishments reported being unionized.

How Has Productivity Been Reflected in Wages?

Mexico is just starting to link productivity to wages. However, this productivity-wage link area has recently become a key issue for modernization of management systems.

For more than 30 years, the Constitution and the Federal Labor Law made it compulsory to distribute 10 percent of company profits to workers. In practice, however, the result has been a system of cash payments that are interpreted as wage supplements and are not clearly linked to productivity.

In 1992, just 4.3 percent of wages in the manufacturing sector corresponded to explicit recognition of employee efforts or attitudes (STPS 1995). This type of bonus was generally paid to employees who had good punctuality and attendance records, while bonuses for productivity or quality were very infrequent. However, the country was interested in undertaking a joint effort in this area, which led the main unions, the employers' associations, and the government in 1993 to sign a national agreement on the improvement of quality and productivity. The agreement promoted discussion and awareness of the issue and analyzed the main structural problems in each sector. However, it has been more difficult to make headway in translating concepts and lines of action into practical systems applicable to the specific situations in companies. How should productivity be measured? What practices should be encouraged? How should increases in productivity be linked to wages?

In 1994, only a year after the accord was signed, 50.7 percent of wage negotiations between companies and unions under federal jurisdiction included agreements to pay financial incentives for productivity (STPS 1994). Those agreements covered 1.2 million employees, or 78 percent of workers involved in collective bargaining on the federal level (generally companies with more than 300 employees).

Unlike in the 1992 survey, punctuality and attendance in 1994 ceased to be the first items taken into account when paying incentives. They were replaced with the concept of efficiency, which included reductions in downtime, waste, substandard production, and savings of resources. Punctuality and attendance came second, and some companies combined them with other factors for measuring performance. In 89.7 percent of the contracts signed in 1994, incentives took the form of a percentage of the wage. In two-thirds of the cases, evaluations were general, and in 20 percent they were based on individual performance indicators.

In 1995—the year of the crisis—the number of employees benefiting from productivity agreements in the federal jurisdiction fell by the significant figure of 577,000, to 48 percent of those covered in the previous year.

Conclusion

As a result of trade liberalization, the issue of productivity began to be taken seriously by Mexican companies and workers. In some cases productivity became a defense against competition, which caught many companies off guard.

The very concept of productivity has been the subject of a heated debate, which reflects the many different interpretations given to the term by employees, companies, and the government. Initially, each of the players saw productivity as an effort that should basically be made by the others. Employers stressed the need for better training, attitudes, and efforts by employees and demanded that the government simplify its regulatory framework. Workers demanded access to more modern machinery and installations, to higher incentives, to recognition of their efforts, and to better working conditions. The government stressed the need that businesses have a more enterprising attitude to be in tune with the new international context. Convergence of those views and recognition of the need for a change in attitudes, skills, and organization have been a gradual process, as has been the establishment of mechanisms to distribute the benefits of productivity among workers, companies, and consumers. Such convergence and recognition are just getting under way in many areas.

Bibliography

Boon, Gerard K. "Assessment of Past and Future Sectorial Labour Productivity and Primary Inputs in the Mexican Manufacturing Industry." México, D.F.: Nacional Financiera, April 1968. Mimeograph.

Dollar, D., and K. Sokoloff. "Dos Caminos de Expansión Industrial: Incremento de la Productividad Manufacturera en México y Corea del Sur, 1960–1980." In *Industria y Trabajo en México*, edited by J. W. Wilkie and J. Reyes Heroles. México, D.F.: UAM–Azcapotzalco, 1990.

Hernández Laos, Enrique. *Evolución de la Productividad Total de los Factores en México*. México, D.F.: Ediciones Productividad, 1973.

———. "Diferenciales de Productividad entre México, Canadá y Estados Unidos." In *Cuadernos del Trabajo*, no. 5. México, D.F.: STPS, 1994a.

———. "Tendencias de la Productividad en México, 1970–1991." In *Cuadernos de Trabajo*, no. 8. México, D.F.: STPS, 1994b.

Secretaría del Trabajo y Prevision Social (STPS). *Reporte de Convenios de Productividad en la Jurisdicción Federal*. México, D.F.: STPS, December 1994.

Secretaría del Trabajo y Prevision Social (STPS), Instituto Nacional de
Estadística Geografía e Informática (INEGI), Organización
Internacional del Trabajo (OIT). *Encuesta Nacional de Empleo,
Salarios, Tecnología y Capacitación en el Sector Manufacturero*. México,
D.F.: STPS, 1995.

World Bank. *Mexico: Trade Policy, Industrial Performance, and Adjustment*. Washington, D.C.: World Bank, 1986.

CHAPTER 10

Comments on Chapters 7, 8, and 9

Carlos Gutiérrez-Ruiz
National President of Canacintra

Comments on Chapter 7, *Changing Employment Relationships in an Open Economy: A Microeconomic Perspective*

Chapter 7 analyzed the impact of technology and market globalization on labor and discussed the repercussions on productivity and competitiveness of businesses in the context of an open economy and a traditional economy. In this respect, the author, Ray Marshall, notes that the more traditional contexts—rather than competitive markets—generally emphasize political and social stability at the national level.

Proof of this observation lies in the fact that companies that are controlled by the state are generally less competitive at the international level than are companies regulated by market forces. Similarly, the document points out that the regulatory and collective bargaining processes are more difficult to maintain in an open economy.

With respect to the challenge of competitiveness, it is worth noting that success in an open economy requires companies, individuals, and governments to develop competitive strategies. In this regard, Marshall notes that in traditional national economies, emphasis is placed on the sources of physical resources; the social and political objectives for economic organization; the stability through laws, regulations, and contracts; and the policies and controls of the national economy.

By contrast, the author notes that in a more open economy, greater attention is paid to quality, productivity in the use of all resources, international economies of scale, and development of human capital.

In this sense, the productivity of companies in open economies translates into an important factor with respect to competition, which should go hand-in-hand with higher quality products at competitive prices. Lower costs should be achieved directly by reducing prices or wages or indirectly by improving productivity or the product per unit of input.

With respect to quality, Marshall notes that open systems are more focused on the consumer while traditional systems, which are less competitive, are more focused on the producer.

Flexibility in production is also important because it constitutes a reward related to the speed at which consumer needs are met and the speed at which changes occur in the market and technology.

The microeconomic implication is that companies that wish to be viable in a given country must focus on flexibility and on value added for all production factors in the long term.

With respect to public policy, the competitiveness strategies adopted by companies have significant implications for the public well-being. The option of reducing direct costs means salary and employment problems for many workers, along with unequal growth in wages and incomes. Such unequal growth threatens the stability of democratic and social institutions.

One problem for public policy is that the option for achieving high value added requires a strategy. In many situations, a pure internal market strategy should stimulate a cost-reduction strategy. Therefore, interventions are required to spur companies along the road to achieving value-added strategies. Such interventions include policies that would do the following:

1. Stimulate fair and effective competition.

2. Improve quality and reduce the cost of goods, services, and production factors.

3. Balance production and consumption.

4. Stimulate the development of science, technology, infrastructure, and human resources.

5. Provide for social security and participation by employees in decisions taken by the company.

6. Ensure legal protection for organizing workers' rights and collective contracts.

Marshall also mentions that a strategy of high value added has clear implications for international economic and political organizations. Questions have been raised as to whether in an open and global economy we should improve upon organizations or mechanisms to raise the standard of living for the entire population. But a set of realities also must be considered in modernizing international policies and organizations. Those realities are as follows:

1. Market forces in themselves do not guarantee sustainable economic systems. Therefore, the markets must operate using transparent and steadfast rules—known as fair play.

2. International policies and organizations should balance the costs and benefits of change. This intervention is necessary above all when taking into account that market forces in themselves would create a lopsided distribution of benefits.

3. A general principle for international organizations and policies should be to seek convergence between better wages and working conditions, which will, in turn, raise lower standards of living rather than lowering higher ones. In other words, organizations and policies could be more viable if they were based on measures that encourage all countries to adopt strategies of high value added and to minimize measures of direct cost reduction.

4. Labor standards, such as those set out in NAFTA, may play a limited but important role in ensuring that international policies are mutually beneficial. The most important policies are those that increase value added. However, there is no guarantee that workers' salaries will be reflected in higher productivity.

Comments on Chapter 8, *The Challenge of Workplace Innovation in Canada*

In the context of the rapid changes taking place in society, the Canadian public is extremely worried about competition in the labor market and about the lack of labor skills. To a certain extent, the public's misgivings arise from high unemployment rates, low wages, and polarization of income.

However, these worries merely reflect the serious erosion of social and labor institutions under the screen of contracts, employer-employee relationships, and practices in traditional workplaces, as well as government policies that are not geared to the new production conditions.

For the past two generations, these social and labor institutions, along with their long-term employment relations, collective representation, labor regulations, and public safety nets, supported economic security under the objectives of equality and improved economic efficiency.

However, the experience built up by the traditional institutions from the post–World War II period to 1975 could not find a footing when techno-economics and a globalized, integrated, and high-technology economy emerged.

Industrial labor contracts from the era of long-term collective bargaining agreements are undergoing substantial change as the result of innovation, competition, and time requirements of both employers and employees.

The author, Gordon Betcherman, correctly points out that as the traditional tools are becoming less effective, the only certainty is that others must be invented to replace them.

Canada, faced with the challenge of NAFTA, has taken on the task of modernizing public practices and policies in the workplace. This modernization is aimed at improving productivity and income distribution, as well as providing new tools and bases for linking the processes of integration to the well-being of all society.

In reviewing the experiences that have led to the economic uncertainty of Canadians, Betcherman makes it clear that the phenomenon is not unique to that country. The economic changes that have occurred in almost all countries have prompted similar phenomena among workers.

Among the developed countries, Canada has been hardest hit by unemployment resulting from steady cutbacks in public spending. In addition, apprehension was created during the 1980s by the sharp fluctuations and the conditions that prevailed in the labor market. By contrast, in the 1990s employment is practically impervious to fluctuations and flows in the economy.

From a more individual point of view, the author indicates that the uncertainty results not only from major economic changes, but also from changes in labor rules in the various jobs. For example, social assistance is being gradually eliminated.

Thus, the uncertainty of Canadians relates to the impact felt by individuals and society as a whole upon realizing that the market provides them with lower levels of security and with fewer social benefits. People have become less confident in these tempestuous times of changing rules in the labor world.

The three key issues in the debate on the current situation and on trends in the Canadian labor market are unemployment, wages and benefits, and new employment rules.

The problem of unemployment has become more complex. The seasonal effects of the economic cycle have been added to structural components. In general, the displacement of workers by the inclusion of new technologies and by economic restructuring has increased.

Furthermore, wages have stagnated owing to the lack of clear rules for measuring performance, especially in the service sector; the loss of bargaining power by employees who have had to sacrifice wages for work; and the inflexibility of some workers who refuse to play by the new labor rules that productivity demands.

Government promotion programs that give greater support to women are one factor in the polarization of incomes. Another factor is the entry of young workers who are hired at lower wages and for longer hours of work. Also, a growing number of Canadians are willing to work more than the usual 35 to 40 hours per week, even on a short-term basis. In general terms, these phenomena partly explain the polarization of worker income mentioned earlier. All of this polarization is the result of modernization and technological changes, as well as changes that have come in their wake among work organizations.

On the micro level, the discussion is important in two senses. First, the rules in workplaces are changing. Such changes have an impact on workers by creating uncertainty. Second, certain economic and labor market trends are requiring economic units to make new changes in their labor strategies.

Labor relations have had to become more flexible as a result of technological issues, competition requirements, and higher rates of unemployment. In addition, workers have had to take part in training processes that equip them with better skills for adapting to the changing tasks that a specific job now demands.

Betcherman notes that organizational strategies in North America take on the forms known as the "center-periphery" and "supported production" models. Such strategies are aimed at boosting the product's quality and the speed of manufacture and at offering suitable maintenance and repair services, which are aspects that the market and competition demand.

Organizational changes have different impacts on individuals. They generate polarization and strong competition among workers, and they lead to deep segmentation of the labor market. In addition, investments in human capital are focused on more highly skilled workers (the center), and there is a gap between them and less-skilled workers (the periphery). This gap leads to polarization of income and generates significant uncertainty throughout the labor market.

All of these changes resulting from technological modernization, growth of competition, and globalization have had a direct impact on the forms of production and labor organization. The lack of flexibility demonstrated by unions in coping with these changes has also generated more uncertainty in the working class in Canada.

Today, some labor unions are seeking to adapt to the changes and are trying to recoup some of the labor benefits they had under the old system. However, this process is still too slow, since in most cases the interests of employees and employers are distinct. One group wants greater productivity, and the other group wants better working conditions.

The author indicates that it is necessary to use new social consensuses (workers, entrepreneurs, and government) to revitalize and seek new forms of reactivating the social contract in the postindustrial era. This strategy appears to be sound.

Comments on Chapter 9, *Technological Change, Trade Liberalization, and Change in the Business Climate in Mexico*

The concept of productivity is more than a simple technical combination of the various production factors that help a company meet the needs of its clients by providing an efficient supply of services and products. Today more than ever, productivity is a social relationship between production agents, and it goes beyond mere economic quantification.

In this sense, productivity is the means an economy can use to achieve high levels of competitiveness, improve the chances that the goods and services it produces can compete in terms of quality and price on international markets, and ensure that this positioning in the market guarantees a better standard of living for the nation as a whole.

One important point made by the author, Norma Samaniego-Breach, is the lack of strategic planning of the economic development process in Mexico's manufacturing industry. The underuse of factors in the production process helped create the paradox of high growth rates in the gross domestic product, while at the same time the total factor productivity grew at a more modest rate.

One of the main explanations of why the productivity parameter has not attained international levels lies in the process of interaction, organization, and management. That process persists among the different production agents in Mexico. I am referring specifically to relationships among the various federal institutions and among them and businesses and workers.

To expand, empirical evidence shows that, at least in the beginning, trade liberalization has in itself been incapable of increasing the total productivity levels of factors in Mexican industry, as demonstrated by data for the years 1980 to 1990. In this sense, mere exposure to greater competition from foreign products and services has not in itself ensured efficiency or optimal use of production processes.

The toy industry, which suffered from mass closures as a result of such exposure, is a costly example of the impact that a process of trade liberalization can have in the absence of tools that will assist businesses in moving toward production with higher levels of quality and productivity, more innovative supervision, more efficient labor management systems, and more flexible production processes. When an economy lacks the internal production relations needed to transform the challenge of trade liberalization into a genuine opportunity, problems result.

Of course, some winners have emerged in this natural selection process, as mentioned in the chapter. However, they are in the minority because of breaks in production chains resulting from the absence of an industrial policy that promotes opportunities for our companies to conquer new markets.

Conclusion

All of the above information shows us what type of organizational tissue a society must have, first to support productivity and then to work toward the competitiveness of its companies and of the economy as a whole. For that reason, productivity requires mechanisms for social cohesion and support for individual action through the coordination of production factors. We might call this the institutional basis that serves as the springboard for achieving the full use of productive factors.

Proof of this need lies in the status of innovation, adaptation, and dissemination in Mexico, because success stories in this area have shown that networks of institutional relations are necessary if a project is to be successful. The project usually must have access to financing under adequate terms and to the know-how of technological development centers. Businesses must also show the determination to achieve technological levels that are consistent with demand.

One of the obstacles to productivity is that not all companies have statistical parameters that they can use as a continuous yardstick to measure performance. Not surprisingly, the large companies have created parameters to evaluate their own progress, but medium-sized and small businesses are lagging well behind in achieving this goal. As the text indicates, the larger companies base their productivity strategies on new supervisory frameworks, and the smaller companies base their strategies on job rotation systems—differing approaches that shed a great deal of light on the microeconomic performance of businesses, depending on their size.

The challenge that lies ahead is to be able to advance toward the differentiated promotion of branches of industry or businesses at the regional level, because cultural, geographic, educational, and historical factors have helped explain the varying levels of industrialization within countries such as Italy and Germany. Along these lines, reviews of sectoral cases of productivity must progress toward a level that combines the greatest number of explanations of this phenomenon.

A more active role by employees in decision making and an improvement in employer-employee relations were present in 80 percent of the cases in which productivity levels increased—a situation that places the labor factor at the center of the debate on productivity. I, therefore, agree with the statement that views the equitable distribution of the profits generated by productivity as part of the great challenge of moving from a measurement parameter, called "productivity," to a category of collective benefit that could be called "competitiveness."

To this end, we must boost the potential of the labor force as an investment more than as an expense. This approach means visualizing wages as an engine for the virtuous cycle of growth and not as a cost.

CHAPTER 11

Comments on Chapter 8

Gérald Larose
President of the Confederation of National Trade Unions (CSN)

Introduction

It is with pleasure that the CSN is taking part in the first seminar on incomes and productivity organized by the Commission for Labor Cooperation.

This is an opportune time to make an initial assessment of the impact caused by implementation of, first, the Canada–United States free trade agreement (CAFTA) and, later, the Canada–Mexico–United States agreement (North American Free Trade Agreement, or NAFTA).

To begin, I would like to outline the effects that implementation of this treaty has had on the economy and employment. I will go on to discuss its impact on labor relations in Canada and Quebec. Finally, I will list the implications for public policy.

Impact on the Economy and Employment

Controversy has raged in Canada and Quebec over the impact that CAFTA and NAFTA have had on the development of the economy and employment in Canada and Quebec. From 1989 to 1993—the first 5 years that CAFTA was in effect—Canada experienced the worst recession of all the G–7 countries. Unemployment soared, while the balance of trade plummeted. Many pointed to the free trade agreements as the main cause of this profound economic turbulence. But, as Professor Trefler asked in chapter 2, how much of this decline can really be attributed to the free trade treaty, or to the monetary policies, or to the recession in other countries, or to the technological revolution, or to the opening up of markets and the increased presence of the Asian bloc? It is not easy to separate the extent of the effects produced by each of these factors.

Since 1995, there has been a gradual, but eventually impressive, restoration of the balance of trade. Three factors account for this turnaround. First, demand from the United States has risen continually, having a substantial effect on imports from Canada. Second, the Canadian dollar has depreciated to a point where the American dollar is consistently worth over 20 percent more. Third, the difference in the inflation rate between Canada and the United States from 1990 to 1996 was seven points. With respect to the economy, the jury is still out; as for the balance of trade, after dropping sharply, it has gradually recovered.

In terms of employment, the situation is completely different. As the experts indicated in previous chapters, we can see significant shrinkage throughout the manufacturing sector. It should also be noted that the unemployment rate in Canada generally hovers at a point about twice the American rate. In addition, inequities in accessibility to employment and wages have continued to rise.

I will not say anything more about the long controversy over the impact of the free trade treaties on the economy and employment except that, as Professors Krueger (chapter 6) and Betcherman (chapter 8) explained, a number of common trends can be seen in the three countries.

Impact on Labor Relations

What consequences has the implementation of the free trade treaties had on labor relations?

First, the new context created by the free trade treaties serves as a new and now steady reference point for management. It has become natural to refer to working conditions in the United States or Mexico. Mention is also routinely made of the substantial differences in the social safety net, in addition to the significantly lower rate of unionization in the United States, particularly in the South, more specifically in what is known as the Sunbelt. The phenomenon of the *maquiladoras* in Mexico since 1994 is another facet of the debate.

There has been less talk about wages, particularly those paid in the United States, since 1994, when the value of the Canadian dollar fell so low in comparison with the U.S. dollar. In concrete terms, the implementation of the free trade treaties has had an impact on labor relations, in that management's benchmarks now systematically include the situations in the United States and Mexico.

Second, it must also be realized that the free trade treaties create opportunities for increased competition with other regions of North America. This is especially the case in the sectors related to natural resources such as the production of lumber, pulp and paper, aluminum, and various other metals. It is also the case with our hydroelectric resources. Sectors in which Canada, and Quebec in particular, stand out in terms of technological innovation (such as aeronautics, public transportation equipment, and pharmaceutical products) are expanding at the same time.

This entire situation has forced the union movement to develop new approaches and new practices, which include the following:

1. Union organizations have devoted more resources to developing a better knowledge of sectors throughout North America.

2. Originally against technological change, the union movement decided to shift to the offense and force businesses to keep up to date in relation to new production processes and technologies.

3. It became evident very quickly that productivity gains that might make the difference between the growth or decline of a business could

not be made without the reorganization of work. The CSN, particularly in the past 7–8 years, has made substantial investments in research, training, and testing to achieve a revolution in a number of industrial sectors primarily through recognition of employees' contributions, enhancement of employees' duties, and standardization of control procedures.

4. Work reorganization also provided an opportunity for many unions to put on the table some proposals that they had been promoting for a number of years and that are aimed at reducing work time.

5. Occupational training, like ongoing training, has become a union priority.

6. The CSN has established its own advisory group on job retention and creation. That group is composed of professionals from all sectors who work with all our unions in the economic monitoring of their company's development.

7. The union movement is also heavily involved in the development of the economic partnership. The creation of workers' funds by the Quebec Federation of Labour and later by the CSN, such as the regrouping of existing credit unions in various workplaces, enabled the unions to become involved in ownership and thus carry some weight in decision making designed to guarantee the future of the businesses.

8. In these past few years, unions have made substantial gains, thereby firmly establishing both participative management and the more extensive influence of workers on a number of decisions relating to the future of their companies.

9. A trend has also developed toward longer collective agreements to guarantee relative labor peace in terms of major investments or restructuring.

10. The CSN in particular has also invested a great deal of energy in organizing self-employed workers in nontraditional areas, notably in the culture sector and the field of alternative medicine.

We can conclude this second section by noting that the implementation of the free trade treaty has had both negative and positive effects on labor relations in that it has forced the union movement to be innovative in its objectives, strategies, and means of operating in order to carry out its union mandate.

Impact on Public Policy

My final point concerns the impact of the free trade treaty on public policy.

When asking whether the free trade treaty is a good or a bad thing and whether there are any winners or losers, Professor Trefler (chapter 2) told us that the answer depended on the type of social assistance provided for victims of the free trade agreement. If that is the criterion on which we have to base our judgment, I would conclude that in Canada it has been a dismal failure. Despite the promises of the Conservative government at the time, no preparation, transition, or compensation program was introduced following ratification of the free trade treaty, contrary to what was and is being done in the United States. What is more, we have to say that the government seems determined to amend all of our social policies to bring them in line with those in the United States. The most recent was the reform of unemployment insurance, hypocritically now called employment insurance, which in actual fact allows less than 45 percent of the contributors to the fund who are unemployed to collect benefits, when prior to the reform, 90 percent of unemployed workers were entitled to such benefits.

It should also be noted that, when major changes in all industrial sectors were generated with the implementation of these treaties, the long dispute regarding responsibility and resources available for occupational training was not resolved. Still today the federal government contradicts Quebec's approach regarding an active labor market policy.

Professor Betcherman (chapter 8) told us that while flexibility had become necessary to face competition, it had to be accompanied by security backed up by some form of social support. In the absence of such support, major resistance has to be expected, as Professor Marshall (chapter 7) indicated. When we see that the employment insurance fund generates a surplus of billions of dollars—there will be $18 billion by the end of 1998—and that this surplus merely goes toward paying off the deficit of the Minister of Finance, we have to realize that Canada is heading in the wrong direction and is, therefore, compromising the movement required in the various industrial and service sectors.

In Canada, I think that we can easily draw the conclusion that the liberalization of the market and the openness allowed by the free trade treaties have so far merely served to make the entire structure of social programs consistently weak.

Conclusion

I hope that we can learn from the European experience and expand the opening made in the free trade treaties by the side agreements on labor and the environment. These side agreements are a starting point for us. We feel that markets cannot be opened up unless international guarantees are introduced concerning the minimum conditions to be put in place in the three countries regarding democratic, union, social, compensation, and labor rights.

The CSN is specifically proposing that seven International Labour Organization conventions be included in the existing treaty, in the future treaty covering all the Americas, or in the World Trade Organization Agreement. The United States waged a huge battle to introduce the recognition of intellectual property rights, sanctionable commercially, in the World Trade Organization Agreement. We do not see why the right to freedom of association set out in Convention 87 of the Agreement, the right to organize and bargain collectively in Convention 98, the prohibition against forced or compulsory labor in Conventions 29 and 105, the right to equal remuneration for men and women in Convention 100, the prohibition against discrimination in Convention 111, and the recognition of a minimum age for employment in Convention 138 would be any less sanctionable commercially than intellectual property rights. For us, the opening up of markets cannot be achieved solely and strictly through a laissez-faire approach. Market openness may be profitable for all populations, particularly for workers and all of the working class. This is a union matter, but it is also a social concern. It is up to us to press our political leaders to implement these international standards, which have been ratified by all members of the tripartite International Labour Organization.

These, in short, are a few aspects to be considered regarding the impact of the free trade treaties on the labor community in Quebec and Canada.

CHAPTER 12

Comments on Chapter 9

Gilberto Muñoz-Mosqueda
Union of Workers in the Chemical, Petrochemical,
Carbon-Chemical, and Related Industries in the Republic of Mexico

Information presented at the North American Seminar on Incomes and Productivity will undoubtedly shed new light on the behavior and evolution of the concept of productivity and competitiveness in labor markets, as well as on the changing labor relations in an open economy such as the one that applies today. In this new international economic model, legal and contractual rules will play a role in finding good solutions in a new business-labor context that will need to adjust to the rapid changes under way in the working world, especially in the NAFTA member countries—Canada, Mexico, and the United States.

The degrees of influence that workers have, as well as workers' levels of representation and participation, depend on the types of industries involved and are clearly significant for progress.

As a result, it is necessary to modernize workplace practices through means that contribute to both productivity and better distribution of income, which will, on the one hand, ensure company survival and competitiveness, and, on the other hand, ensure worker development and benefits.

New opportunities for production are erasing the borders of space and time, and many traditional organizations have fallen behind. Around the world, organizations are now embarking on a sweeping process of change in their organizational frameworks.

In Mexico, special note should be taken of union, business, and government participation in various lively forums such as the Agreement for Economic Development, the National Advisory Committee on Health and Safety in the Workplace, the Mexican Council on Competitiveness and Productivity, and the Council for Standardization and Certification of Employee Skills.

The Union of Workers in the Chemical, Petrochemical, Carbon-Chemical, and Related Industries in the Republic of Mexico, which I represent, has long agreed with business that fundamental elements are international competitiveness, the culture of effectiveness, quality systems, and safety in the workplace. These elements support the mission, vision, policies, and quality objectives of business as they guarantee the permanence and growth of jobs by establishing management systems along with modernization, competitiveness, and profitability programs under a framework of mutual understanding and respect. Such elements will help the unions adapt to the new conditions that markets and the business climate will demand in the future. The basic goal will be for both parties to achieve results that ensure survival and competitiveness for existing, new, and future businesses, thus boosting employee development and benefits.

Labor Agreement Goals

Under this framework, the union has clearly defined objectives and programs to steer these efforts in its collective labor agreements with companies. The areas of opportunity include the following:

1. Culture of effectiveness is a goal of labor and management to ensure that workers focus their efforts on achieving results, while striking a balance among human development, human nature, and potential, as

well as meeting the needs of modernity and maintaining an open and proactive attitude toward change.

2. Organizational quality is a result that both labor and management are committed to achieving through projects to improve the industry, thereby meeting needs and making the most of opportunities.

3. Competitive cost is the economic expression of the results of production as sold in the marketplace.

4. A better quality of life, a result sought by the union, includes achieving conditions that favor worker productivity and development. Such conditions would incorporate and analyze the physical conditions of facilities, integration activities, employee participation, incentives and remuneration systems, the main standards for health and safety in the workplace, and increased productivity. The results of these efforts would express the dynamism of a company by comparing its results with the best international practices.

In addition, the union has agreed with the companies with which it maintains labor relations: a labor model associated with the principles of total quality will be included in collective contracts. This model will help meet the needs of technological modernization and international standards. It will incorporate operating and management systems into the culture of each business.

The Importance of Quality of Life

The labor model holds that one basic principle of companies is that workers should be able to achieve quality of life in their work by developing their skills and individual potential. The training for this purpose should develop a work culture whose central values are productivity, quality, safety, and development, on both the institutional and individual levels. It should be geared to profiles at each level and should include skills relating to teamwork, problem solving, and safety and hygiene, all of which should be applied in the process of total quality in the workplace.

The framework under which the labor model integrates the entire organization is based on the following four points:

1. Leadership covers the various management levels, together with the union and the company.

2. A system links information and analysis through the following:

- A database for decision making that supports the measurement of the targets set
- A labor plan that is aimed at achieving international competitiveness and that takes the performance of the world economy into account
- A national development plan and a strategic plan for the labor sector
- Employee development that includes promoting and optimizing the potential of workers on an ongoing basis and gives them decision-making authority within the work team
- Administration and improvement of the processes that guide the operation of the organization
- Assessment of the impact on society, which looks at whether companies make continuing efforts to improve their physical, social, economic, and environmental surroundings
- The inclusion of international quality standards

3. The goal implies quality that is based on giving better value to clients.

4. Progress is measured through the analysis of indicators related to the system and the goal.

In today's world, more participation is required from workers in order to rehabilitate the national economy and to establish optimal wage-price graphs. I feel strongly that cooperation from workers is necessary to coordinate efforts with government programs aimed at more extensive industrialization, which will allow capital investors to create more jobs. However, at the same time, we must demand fair wages and better training programs in order to increase productivity and consequently to obtain a higher economic level.

We agree with the statement by Norma Samaniego-Breach (chapter 9) regarding the importance of changes in attitudes, skills, and forms of organization, along with the need for mechanisms that help distribute the benefits of productivity among workers, businesses, and consumers.

The Union of Workers in the Chemical, Petrochemical, Carbon-Chemical, and Related Industries in the Republic of Mexico has embarked on this path in the conviction that Mexican labor-relations laws are not, and have never been, a barrier to allowing production factors to work for the benefit of society and of our country as a whole.

About the Speakers

José Luis Alberro-Semerena

José Luis Alberro-Semerena is currently chairman and CEO of Diseño de Estrategias, a management and financial consulting firm.

In 1995, Dr. Alberro was chief of staff, Secretary's Office, in the Department of Commerce and Industrial Policy of Mexico. In this capacity, he supported development of the Mexican Trade and Industry Policy Program. From 1992 to 1994, he was president and CEO (general director) of Pemex-Gas and Basic Petrochemicals. He has held various positions in Petroleos Mexicanos (Pemex) and was a member of the Mexican Negotiating Group to NAFTA.

Dr. Alberro has also held these public positions in the Mexican Department of Budgeting and Planning: chief economic adviser to the Secretary of Planning and Budget (1988) and senior economist and project administrator (1986–1987). From 1989 to 1990, he was senior economist and regional adviser in Economic Development for the Economic Commission for Latin America and the Caribbean; and from 1986 to 1990, he was a consultant to the World Bank.

Dr. Alberro was assistant professor in the Department of Economics at the University of Illinois at Chicago during 1978–1982. He also was professor in the Centro de Estudios Económicos of El Colegio de México (COLMEX) during 1982–1992. In the COLMEX, he was funding director of a specialized journal, "Economic Studies of El Colegio de México," as well as of a collection of research papers called "Working Papers," both edited by El Colegio de México.

For several years, Dr. Alberro was a member of the Scientist Research Academy at the Universidad Nacional Autónomo de México (UNAM), the American Economic Association, and the Econometric Society. He was also a member of the editorial board of the *Journal Economic Tri-Monthly* and the *Magazine of Statistics*.

Dr. Alberro received his B.A. in economics from the Instituto Tecnológico Autónomo de México (ITAM), and his M.A. and Ph.D. in economics from the University of Chicago.

Steven M. Beckman

Since June 1985, Steven M. Beckman has been responsible for developing United Auto Workers (UAW) positions and policies on all aspects of international trade and investment issues. He represents the UAW in meetings with officials in executive branch agencies; with members of Congress and their staff; and with various business, academic, government, and general audiences on international trade and related issues. He has been involved in major trade negotiations (Uruguay Round, United States–Japan Framework, NAFTA) and legislation through testimony before House and Senate committees on behalf of the UAW.

In addition, Mr. Beckman is involved in UAW international affairs activities and has met with union representatives and workers from countries around the world, including Japan, Brazil, Mexico, South Africa, France, Australia, and Germany. He has represented the UAW in international meetings on the impact of international economic policies on workers and on international standards for workers' rights.

He is a member of several government advisory committees on international trade: Labor Advisory Committee for Trade Negotiations and Trade Policy (U.S. Department of Labor), Auto Parts Advisory Committee (U.S. Department of Commerce), and International Economic Policy Advisory Committee (U.S. Department of State). He began his work with the labor movement in 1976 as an intern in the AFL–CIO Research Department. He went on to the International Union of Electrical Workers (IUE) and the Industrial Union Department of the AFL–CIO, where he worked on international trade, technological change, and collective bargaining.

Mr. Beckman received his B.A. from Harvard University and an M.A. in economics from the University of Massachusetts.

Gordon Betcherman

As executive director of the Human Resource Group at Ekos Research Associates and director of the Work Network of the Canadian Policy Research Networks, Gordon Betcherman is responsible for large research programs in the area of labor market and human resource analysis. Most recently, he has completed a major project on employment and training as well as studies on the future of work, workplace innovation, and youth employment.

During 1992–1994, Dr. Betcherman was a senior fellow in the School of Industrial Relations at Queen's University. There he directed a major study on human resource management trends, which culminated in the publication of *The Canadian Workplace in Transition*. From 1987 to 1992, he was a research director at the Economic Council of Canada, where he was responsible for a number of research studies, one of which was Good Jobs, Bad Jobs, and Employment in the Service Economy.

Dr. Betcherman has written widely in Canadian, American, and European publications on a range of economic and social issues. He is currently co-editor of *Canadian Business Economics*, a visiting fellow at the School of Policy Studies at Queen's University, a member of the Statistics Canada Advisory Committee on Labour Statistics, and a director of the Canadian Policy Research Networks and the Canadian Workplace Research Network. He is a frequent commentator on labor and social trends at policy, academic, and business conferences and in the media.

Dr. Betcherman received his doctorate from the University of California at Los Angeles, with earlier degrees from the University of Toronto and Carleton University.

Carroll E. Bostic

Carroll E. Bostic began her career with Eastman Kodak Company in 1978 as a sales representative who marketed radiographic products. She has held a variety of positions within Kodak in different regions of the United States, including managing a group responsible for marketing Kodak products to the federal, state, and local governments.

After joining Kodak's Federal Government Relations staff in May 1992, she became responsible for Human Resources Affairs. She was an adviser to the Employer's Delegate at the 82nd Session of the International Labour Conference in Geneva in June 1995. She was selected by the U.S. Secretary of Labor to sit on the National Administrative Office (NAO) Advisory Committee as a business representative to provide advice for business trade associations and coalitions including U.S. Council on International Business, the Business Roundtable, National Association of Manufacturers, Labor Policy Association, and Electronic Industries Association.

Ms. Bostic was born in Cambridge, Massachusetts. She graduated from and taught in Boston's Northeastern University program of Radiologic Technology as a clinical instructor at one of the local affiliated hospitals. She holds a master's degree in education from Antioch University; a master's degree from Purdue University's Krannert School of Management; and a certificate from the Program for Senior Managers in Government, John F. Kennedy School of Government, Harvard University.

Sam Boutzlouvis

Sam Boutzlouvis is a senior associate for policy and an economist with the Business Council on National Issues (BCNI), which is an Ottawa-based, nonpartisan, not-for-profit organization composed of the chief executive officers of 150 leading corporations in Canada. Formed in

1976, BCNI is the senior voice of Canadian business on public policy issues in Canada and internationally. BCNI engages in an active program of research, consultation, and advocacy. Its focus nationally is to help build a strong economy, and to establish progressive social policies and healthy political institutions. BCNI's global mandate is to ensure that Canadian chief executives play an influential role in the international economic, trade, and foreign affairs domains.

Within the BCNI Secretariat, Mr. Boutzlouvis is responsible for policy analysis research. He plays an active role in support of the Council's Task Force on the National Economy and on matters concerning competitiveness and trade. His responsibilities include supporting the president of BCNI's Task Force on the National Economy in developing strategic global priorities and business-to-business linkages in key world markets for the Council. Mr. Boutzlouvis has been with BCNI for 6 years and has served 2 years as president of the Ottawa Economics Association.

Educated at Carleton University and the University of Ottawa, Mr. Boutzlouvis holds a B.Sc. in biochemistry, a B.A. in economics, and an M.A. in public administration.

Jorge A. de Regil

Jorge de Regil was born in Mexico City and was educated in Mexico City; Windsor, Ontario; and Washington, D.C. He obtained his law degree in 1969.

Mr. de Regil is a senior partner of Baker & McKenzie, S.C. (Mexico), formerly Bufete Sepulveda, S.C., a Mexican law firm established in 1950, and a capital partner of Baker & McKenzie. He is the head of the Labor and Litigation Department.

Since 1985, Mr. de Regil has been the Mexican private sector representative in the Governing Body of the International Labour Office (ILO) in Geneva and titular member of the Freedom of Association Committee of the ILO. He is also president of the General Council (1996–1997) of the International Organization of Employers, also in Geneva. He was a member of the Board of the Mexican Social Security Institute and was for 12 years the chairman of the Labour and

Social Welfare Affairs of CONCAMIN (Mexican Confederation of Industrial Chambers). From 1977 through 1991, he was a titular member of the Mexican Minimum Wage Commission.

Mr. de Regil has been chairman of the Labor Affairs Committee of the American Chamber of Commerce, president of the National Association of Corporate Lawyers, and president of the Mexican Academy on Social Security Studies, as well as a member for the private sector in most of the tripartite bodies of Mexico and the advisory team for NAFTA. He is also a member of the Technical Committee for the New Labor Culture in the Secretariat of Labor of Mexico.

Currently, Mr. de Regil is involved in developing collective bargaining agreements, in interpreting and negotiating those agreements, and in handling government relations. He coordinates the Labor and Practice Group of the Mexican Offices of Baker & McKenzie in Mexico City, Monterrey, Juarez, and Tijuana.

Carlos Gutiérrez-Ruiz

Carlos Gutiérrez-Ruiz is a businessman who undertook specialized studies in enterprise direction and technical topics in the United States and Japan. He is serving as the national president of the National Chamber of the Manufacturing Industry of Mexico (CANACINTRA). He is CEO and staff member of several Mexican enterprises linked to the metal-folding industry and real estate.

Mr. Gutiérrez was vice president of CANACINTRA from 1994 to 1995.

He was the representative at the Enterprise's Organizations Coordination during the negotiation of NAFTA. He was president of the Coordinator Council of the Metal-Mechanic Industry in 1992 and was adviser and president of the metal branch of CANACINTRA from 1988 to 1991.

Andrew Jackson

Andrew Jackson has been a senior economist with the Canadian Labour Congress since May 1989. He has been responsible for

Canadian Labour Congress research on macroeconomic, employment, trade, taxation, and international economic issues. Mr. Jackson is also a research associate of the Canadian Centre for Policy Alternatives. He has written recent major studies on the impacts of free trade on workers and on the future of jobs.

Mr. Jackson was educated at the London School of Economics, where he earned a bachelor's and a master's in economics, and at the University of British Columbia. He has previously worked for the New Democratic Party caucus in British Columbia and in Ottawa, and for the Canadian Labour Market and Productivity Centre.

Alan B. Krueger

Alan B. Krueger is the Bendheim Professor of Economics and Public Affairs at Princeton University. Since 1987, he has held a joint appointment in the Economics Department and Woodrow Wilson School at Princeton. In 1994–1995, he served as chief economist at the U.S. Department of Labor.

He is currently editor of the *Journal of Economic Perspectives*, and a member of the editorial board of the *Quarterly Journal of Economics and Industrial Relations*. He is also the director of the Princeton University Survey Research Center and a research associate of the National Bureau of Economic Research. Dr. Krueger has published widely on the economics of education, technological change, minimum wages, social insurance and environmental economics. He was named a Sloan Fellow in Economics in 1992, and an National Bureau of Economic Research Olin Fellow in 1989–1990. He is a member of the National Academy of Social Insurance.

Dr. Krueger received a B.S. degree with honors from Cornell University's School of Industrial and Labor Relations in 1983, and a Ph.D. in economics from Harvard University in 1987.

Gérald Larose

A social worker at the Hochelaga-Maisonneuve CLSC (local community service center) and an expert in community organization, Gérald

Larose has been, in turn, president of his local union, provincial head of local community service centers for the Social Affairs Federation, information officer at the Montreal Central Council, and president of the Montreal Central Council from 1979 to 1982 before being elected first vice president of the Confederation of National Trade Unions (Confédération des syndicats nationaux, CSN) in June 1982 and president on September 27, 1983. Born in the Eastern Townships of Quebec, the seventh of eleven children of a construction worker, Mr. Larose is the eleventh president of the CSN since it was founded in 1921.

Mr. Larose was instrumental in setting up general associations of students, the federation of general associations of classical colleges (Fédération des associations générales de collèges classiques), and the Quebec Student General Union. He studied theology and social work at the University of Montreal, and he was employed as a teacher and mineral prospector before becoming a social worker.

While serving as first vice president of the CSN, Mr. Larose represented the organization at the Quebec Occupational Health and Safety Research Institute. He was responsible for occupational health and safety, the status of women, and coordination of public- and private-sector bargaining. Since his election as president of the CSN, in addition to his many political duties, he has had the following specific responsibilities: international action, the confederal committee on intercultural relations (Comité confédéral sur les relations interculturelles), the French language, and the information service.

Mr. Larose was a member of the Commission on the Political and Constitutional Future of Quebec, which met in 1990 and 1991. He currently sits on the provincial Advisory Council on Labour and Manpower, plus the Quebec manpower development corporation (Société québécoise de développement de la main d'oeuvre), and he is involved with the Quebec Deposit and Investment Fund.

Mr. Larose is a member of the committee that sponsors the employment forum (Forum pour l'emploi) and represents the CSN in the French Quebec movement (Mouvement Québec Français). He was honored with the "1996 Patriot" medal by the Society of Saint John the Baptist in Montreal.

Ray Marshall

Ray Marshall currently holds the Audre and Bernard Rapoport Centennial Chair in Economics and Public Affairs at the University of Texas, Austin. Mr. Marshall served as U.S. Secretary of Labor under Jimmy Carter. Other positions include member, Commission on the Future of Worker–Management Relations; co-chair, Commission on Skills of the American Workforce; jurist, Heinz Family Foundation Awards; and member, Council on Foreign Relations. Board memberships include German Marshall Fund; Institute for the Future, National Center on Education and the Economy (chair); Industrial Relations Research Association; National Alliance of Business; and USX Corporation (U.S. Steel).

Dr. Marshall has a Ph.D. in economics from the University of California at Berkeley. He is the author of more than 30 books and monographs and approximately 200 articles and chapters. Recent publications include the following:

"Restoring Rural Prosperity." *Rural Cooperatives* (May/June 1996): 26–30.

"Human Resources, Labor Markets, and Economic Performance." In *Political Economy for the 21st Century: Contemporary Views on the Trends of Economics*, edited by Charles J. Whalen, 103–24. Armonk, N.Y.: M. E. Sharpe, 1996.

Worker Participation and Economic Performance: Lessons for the United States. With Brian Turner. Washington, D.C.: Work and Technology Institute, 1995.

"The Global Jobs Crisis." *Foreign Policy* 100 (Fall 1995): 50–68.

"Education, the Economy, and Tomorrow's Workforce." With Robert W. Glover. In *Educating a New Majority: Transforming America's Educational System for Diversity*, edited by Laura I. Rendón and Richard Hope, 35–50. San Francisco: Jossey-Bass Publishers, 1995.

"Work Organization: The Promise of High-Performance Production Systems." In *Reclaiming Prosperity: A Blueprint for Progressive Economic Reform*, edited by Todd Schafer and Jeff Faux. Armonk, N.Y.: M. E. Sharpe, 1995.

"Job and Skill Demands in the New Economy." In *Labor Markets, Employment Policy, and Job Creation*, edited by L. Solman and A. Levenson, 21–57. Boulder, Colo.: Westview, 1994.

"Importance of International Labour Standards in a More Competitive Global Economy." In *International Labour Standards and Economic Interdependence*, edited by Werner Sengenber and Duncan Campbell, 65–79. Geneva: International Institute for Labor Studies, 1994.

"Organizations and Learning Systems for a High-Wage Economy." In *Labor Economics and Industrial Relations: Markets and Institutions*, edited by Clark Kerr. Cambridge, Mass.: Harvard University Press, 1994.

Thinking for a Living: Education and the Wealth of Nations. With Marc Tucker. New York: Basic Books, 1992.

Unheard Voices: Labor and Economic Policy in a Competitive World. New York: Basic Books, 1988.

Gilberto Muñoz-Mosqueda

Gilberto Muñoz-Mosqueda currently holds the following positions: general secretary of the National Executive Committee of the Union of Workers of the Chemical, Petrochemical, Carbon-Chemical, and Related Industries of the Mexican Republic; deputy general secretary of the National Committee of Mexican Confederation of Workers (CTM); and vice president of the Board of Aseguradora Obrera, S.A. (insurance company for workers).

He has been a worker in the fertilizer industry since 1958 (37 years). He is a member of the Board of Instituto del Fondo Nacional de la Vivienda para los Trabajadores (INFONAVIT) (public housing company), member of the Board of the Mexican Social Security (IMSS), and member of the National Advisory Committee in Politics of the PRI (ruling party).

His other activities include the following: Federal Representative in the Congress in the 49th, 51st, and 54th terms; Senator representing the State of Guanajuato in the 52nd and 53rd terms, and Substitute Senator representing the State of Guanajuato in the 56th term.

Charles (Chuck) Nielson

Charles (Chuck) Nielson's work experience began at Thiokol Chemical Corporation in Brigham City, Utah, where he was involved in employment and supervisor training. His next experience was with Fairchild-Hiller Corporation in St. Augustine, Florida, where he supervised industrial relations. He joined Texas Instruments in 1965 and has had a variety of personnel responsibilities including personnel director, Curacao, Netherlands Antilles; personnel director, Consumer Group, Lubbock, Texas; and U.S. personnel manager.

He is currently vice president of Texas Instruments and director of Worldwide Human Resources.

One of his current activities includes being a member of the Executive Committee for the Labor Policy Association (LPA). This group is composed of corporate human resources executives concerned exclusively with the development of the U.S. human resource and employment policies. Mr. Nielson also serves on LPA's Board of Directors.

He was the 1996 chairperson of the Business Roundtable Employee Relations Committee (ERC). The ERC is composed of the top human resource executives at the leading roundtable companies. Working with their respective CEOs, this group plays an active role in legislation affecting the relationship among those companies' employees, employers, and the government.

Mr. Nielson was a member of the Board of Directors for the National Academy of Human Resources (NAHR). He was elected a Fellow of NAHR, Class of 1995. Election as a Fellow to the NAHR is one of the highest honors an individual can achieve in this field. NAHR was founded in 1992 and is dedicated to recognizing individuals for life achievement in human resource management and scholarship. Its program of educational projects and research support advances the work of the profession.

He was appointed in September 1995 to the Dallas County Local Workforce Development Board for a 3-year term. This group is responsible for providing job training and employment opportunities for economically disadvantaged, unemployed persons, and displaced workers throughout the City of Dallas and Dallas County. He was appointed in 1991 by the chancellor to the Board of Visitors for the University of North Texas.

Mr. Nielson received a B.S. degree in sociology from Brigham Young University with minors in psychology and economics. He did graduate work at the University of Utah and Utah State University.

Norma Samaniego-Breach

Norma Samaniego-Breach is an economist who is in charge of Santa Fe Consultores, a consulting firm on economic issues linked with labor matters. She is also professor of labor economics at Iberoamerican University in Mexico City.

She served as secretary of General Comptroller and Administrative Development under President Zedillo's administration from December 1994 to December 1995. Before that position, she undertook a career as public servant, mainly in the labor sector, where she was undersecretary of Labor and Social Welfare from 1991 to 1994. She was the head of the Mexican delegation to the negotiations of the North American Agreement on Labor Cooperation. As the technical secretary of the Welfare, Employment, and Growth Pact (also known as Pacto), she worked on an agreement among government, labor, business, and peasant representatives of Mexico regarding issues related to economic policy, wages, productivity, and employment.

Ms. Samaniego has held other positions in the labor sector, such as president of the National Minimum Wages Commission (a tripartite organization) from December 1988 to December 1990, as well as technical director and alternative director on economic research in this institution. She was underdirector of income distribution and wages at the Secretariat of Labor and Social Welfare (STPS) and adviser for the 1974 National Commission for the Worker's Profit Sharing in the Enterprises. She has worked in the educational public sector, in the Social Security Mexican Institute, and as a researcher at the Graduate Studies Division of the Economics Department of the National Autonomous University of Mexico (UNAM).

Ms. Samaniego graduated from the National Autonomous University of Mexico. She also undertook graduate studies on economic planification in La Haya, Holland.

Adolfo Tena-Morelos

Adolfo Tena-Morelos has 49 years of experience as labor lawyer practitioner and was professor of labor law at the Law Faculty, National Autonomous University of Mexico (UNAM). He is the author of the book *Practical Issues on Training and On-the-Job Training*. He has been lecturer on labor, social security, occupational safety and health, and training issues in domestic and international institutions. He currently serves as president of the Labor Adviser Committee of the Management Confederation of the Republic of Mexico (COPARMEX).

Mr. Tena is a member of the Board of COPARMEX and a member of other committees within the same organization. He also is a member of the Labor Committee of the Mexican Lawyers Bar of the Lawyers College; member of the Labor Committee of the Mexican Confederation of Industrial Chambers (CONCAMIN); member of the Labor Committee of the Mexican Mining Chamber; member of the Mexican Minimum Wage Commission (CONASAMIN); management representative in the CONASAMIN; member of the National Advisory Committee on Employment, Training, and Productivity; member of the Third and Fourth National Commission for Firm's Profit Sharing; CEO of the Strategy Proposals Institute; and a management representative to the National Commission for Firm's Profit Sharing.

In addition, he is a member of the Management Advisory Team for NAFTA negotiations; member of the Mexican Advisory Committee on NAALC; member of the Labor Commission of the Management Coordinator Council (CCE); and a member of the Commission of Productivity and Training of the CCE. Mr. Tena is professor of graduate studies at Pan-American University in Mexico City and professor at Guadalajara University.

Mr. Tena obtained his B.A. in law at the Law Faculty from the National Autonomous University of Mexico.

Daniel Trefler

Daniel Trefler was a tenured faculty member at the Harris Graduate School of Public Policy at the University of Chicago from 1994 to 1996. He recently returned to the Department of Economics at the University of Toronto. He is a research associate at both the National Bureau of Economic Research in Boston and the Institute for Policy Analysis at the University of Toronto.

His research interests are twofold. His first interest is policy-oriented research on the effect of international economic linkages on domestic labor markets. Examples of recent papers include a study of the effects of trade and immigration on U.S. labor markets commissioned by the U.S. Congressional Commission on Immigration Reform, a study of the benefits of Asia–Pacific Economic Cooperation (APEC) commissioned by Industry Canada, and numerous published studies of the impact of the Canada–United States Free Trade Agreement on Canadian labor markets.

The second area of research deals with the appropriate theoretical and empirical modeling of international trade flows and international productivity differences. Examples of recent publications include the following:

"The Case of the Missing Trade and Other Mysteries." *American Economic Review* (December 1995).

"International Factor Price Differences: Leontief Was Right!" *Journal of Political Economy* (December 1993).

"Trade Liberalization and the Theory of Endogenous Protection: An Econometric Study of U.S. Import Policy." *Journal of Political Economy* (February 1993).

Dr. Trefler continues his work on the sources of international productivity and wage differences.

Dr. Trefler obtained his B.A. at the University of Toronto in 1982, his M.Phil. at Cambridge University in 1983, and his Ph.D. at University of California at Los Angeles in 1989.

Edward N. Wolff

Edward N. Wolff is currently professor of economics at New York University, where he has taught since 1974. He serves as managing editor

212

of the *Review of Income and Wealth*, research associate of the Jerome Levy Economics Institute, council member of the International Input-Output Association, associate editor of *Structural Change and Economic Dynamics*, and Editorial Board Member of *Economic Systems Research*. He is a past council member of the International Association for Research in Income and Wealth and has acted as a consultant with the Economic Policy Institute and the World Bank.

His principal research areas are productivity growth, plus income and wealth distribution. He is the author of the following:

Top Heavy: A Study of Increasing Inequality of Wealth in America. New York: Twentieth Century Fund, 1995.

Competitiveness, Convergence, and International Specialization. With David Dollar. Cambridge: MIT Press, 1993.

The Information Economy: The Implications of Unbalanced Growth. With Lars Osberg and William Baumol. Halifax, Nova Scotia: The Institute for Research on Public Policy, 1989.

Productivity and American Leadership: The Long View. With William Baumol and Sue Anne Batey. Cambridge: MIT Press, 1989.

Growth, Accumulation, and Unproductive Activity: An Analysis of the Postwar U.S. Economy. New York: Cambridge University Press, 1987.

He is the editor of the following:

Convergence of Productivity: Cross-National Studies and Historical Evidence. With William Baumol and Richard Nelson. New York: Oxford University Press, 1994.

Poverty and Prosperity in the USA in the Late Twentieth Century. With Dimitri B. Papadimitriou. New York: Macmillan, 1993.

Research in Economic Inequality, Vol. 4. Greenwich, Conn.: JAI Press, 1993.

International Perspectives on Profitability and Accumulation. With Fred Moseley. Aldershot Hants, England: Edward Elgar Publishing Ltd., 1992.

International Comparisons of the Distribution of Household Wealth. New York: Oxford University Press, 1987.

He is also the author of many articles published in books and professional journals. Mr. Wolff received his Ph.D. from Yale University in 1974.

APPENDIX B

Seminar Attendees

(Organizations Named for Identification Purposes Only)

Name	Organization	Country
José L. Alberro-Semerena	Diseño de Estrategias, S.C.	Mexico
Juan P. Arroyo	Universidad Nacional Autónoma de México	Mexico
Miguel Balderas	Nhumo, S.A. de C.V.	Mexico
Steven M. Beckman	United Auto Workers, Washington, D.C.	United States
Graciela Bensusan	Facultad Latinoamericana de Ciencias Sociales	Mexico
Gordon Betcherman	Ekos Research Associates, Inc.	Canada
Armando Beteta	The NAFTA Center, Dallas	Mexico
Leonard Bierman	Texas A&M University	United States
Carroll E. Bostic	Eastman Kodak Co.	United States
Sam Boutzlouvis	Business Council on National Issues	Canada
Jose A. Bouzas	Universidad Nacional Autónoma de México	Mexico

Octavio M. Carvajal	Carvajal Asesores, Concamin	Mexico
Celso Castañeda	Cementos de Chihuahua	Mexico
Jennie Chase	University of North Texas, Denton	United States
Lance Compa	Commission for Labor Cooperation, Secretariat	United States
Kevin Coon	Baker & McKenzie, Toronto	Canada
Hector Cortinas	Texas Instruments, Inc.	United States
Bruce Cranford	U.S. Department of Labor, Dallas	United States
Jeong Dai Kim	University of Texas, Dallas	United States
Maria Demello	University of Texas, Dallas	United States
Jorge A. de Regil	Baker & McKenzie, CONCAMIN	Mexico
Peter Dorman	Michigan State University, East Lansing	United States
Ron Douglas	Teamsters, Canada	Canada
Warren Edmondson	Human Resources Development Ministry	Canada
Dawn R. Elliott	Texas Christian University, Fort Worth	United States
Betty Evans	University of Texas, Dallas	United States
Rómulo Galicia	Comisión Federal de Competencia	Mexico
Raúl Garza	Desarollo Laboral, S.A. de C.V.	Mexico
Burton Gazzara	Commission for Labor Cooperation, Secretariat	
Anthony Giles	Laval University, Quebec	Canada
William Glade	University of Texas, Austin	United States
Holly Gonzalez	U.S.–Mexico Chamber of Commerce	United States
Miguel Gonzalez	Universidad Nacional Autónoma de México	Mexico
Eric Griego	Commission for Labor Cooperation, Secretariat	
Elizabeth Gutiérrez	Universidad Nacional Autónoma de México	Mexico
Carlos Gutiérrez-Ruiz	Cámara Nacional de la Industria de la Transformación	Mexico
Sheila G. De Piñeires	University of Texas, Dallas	United States
Javier Hatch	Girsa Corporativo, S.A. de C.V.	Mexico
Alfredo Hernández	Commission for Labor Cooperation, Secretariat	

Claudio Hernández	Secretaría del Trabajo y Previsión Social	Mexico
Gonzalo Hernández	Instituto Tecnológico Autónomo de México	Mexico
Juan Hernández	University of Texas, Dallas	United States
Jose H. Holguín	Cementos de Chihuahua	Mexico
Andrew Jackson	Canadian Labour Congress	Canada
Rubén Jaén	Cementos de Chihuahua	Mexico
Pedro P. Juárez	Girsa Corporativo, S.A.	Mexico
William Keller	Clark, West, Keller, Butler, & Ellis	United States
Rita Kelly	University of Texas, Dallas	United States
Vincent Kelly	University of Texas, Dallas	United States
Kathy Kopinak	University of Western Ontario, London, Ontario	Canada
Alan B. Krueger	Princeton University	United States
Leoncio Lara	Commission for Labor Cooperation, Secretariat	
Gérald Larose	Confédération de Syndicats Nationaux, Québec	Canada
Gabriela R. López	Instituto de Capacitación de la Industria de la Construcción	Mexico
Darren Lauzon	Human Resources Development Ministry	Canada
Antonio Lozada	Secretaría de Comunicaciones y Transportes	Mexico
Linda Luber	University of Texas, Dallas	United States
Ray Marshall	University of Texas, Austin	United States
Dalil Maschino	Commission for Labor Cooperation, Secretariat	
Isac Maya	Sindicato de Trabajadores de la Industria Química, Petroquímica, Carboquímica, Similares y Conexos de la República Mexicana	Mexico
John McKennirey	Commission for Labor Cooperation, Secretariat	
Michael McPherson	University of North Texas, Denton	United States
Esmeralda Medallín	Univision, Dallas	United States
Arnulfo Méndez	Desarrollo Laboral, S.A. de C.V.	Mexico

Penny Miller	Commission for Labor Cooperation, Secretariat	
Marcus Montalvo	Baker & McKenzie, Dallas	United States
May Morpaw	Human Resources Development Ministry	Canada
Gilberto Muñoz-Mosqueda	Sindicato de Trabajadores de la Industria Química, Petroquímica, Carboquímica, Similares y Conexos de la República Mexicana	Mexico
Allen Myerson	*New York Times*, Dallas	United States
Charles (Chuck) Nielson	Texas Instruments, Inc.	United States
Jesús Nieto	Mexican General Consulate, Dallas	Mexico
Dolores Nieto	Diseño de Estrategias, S.C.	Mexico
Denise Nuno	*Texas Hispanic Journal*	United States
Jim Nykoluk	Manitoba Department of Labour	Canada
Timm O'Leary	*Dallas Morning News*	United States
José Ortiz	Desarollo Laboral, S.A. de C.V.	Mexico
María de los A. Orvañanos	Econo Consultores, S.A. de C.V.	Mexico
Dolores Ozuna	Commission for Labor Cooperation, Secretariat	
Vincent Panvini	Sheet Metal Workers International Association	United States
Hyo Park	University of Texas, Dallas	United States
Rodolfo Perdomo	Cámara Nacional de las Industrias Azucarera y Alcoholera	Mexico
Jim Piatt	U.S. Customs, Dallas	United States
Elias Reyes	University of Texas, Dallas	United States
Jesús Rojas	Cementos de Chihuahua	Mexico
Diego R. Ruiz	Departamento del Distrito Federal	Mexico
Marcelle Saint-Arnaud	Commission for Labor Cooperation, Secretariat	
Fernando Salcedo	Asociación Nacional de la Industria Química, A.C.	Mexico
Norma Samaniego-Breach	Consultores Santa Fe and Universidad Iberoamericana	Mexico
Pablo Sánchez	Instituto Mexicano del Seguro Social	Mexico
Gregory Schoepfle	U.S. Department of Labor	United States
Harley Shaiken	University of California at Berkeley	United States

Dolores Simms	Commission for Labor Cooperation, Secretariat	
Paula K. Simpson	U.S. Customs, Dallas	United States
Esther Skinner	Dallas Chamber of Commerce	United States
Russell E. Smith	Washburn University, Topeka	United States
Felipe Sosa	Cementos de Chihuahua	Mexico
Adolfo Tena-Morelos	Natividad Abogados, S.C., COPARMEX	Mexico
Daniel Trefler	University of Toronto and University of Chicago	Canada
Jorge Vargas	University of Texas, Dallas	United States
Lucinda Vargas	Federal Reserve Bank of Dallas	United States
Wim Vijverberg	University of Texas, Dallas	United States
María Elena Vicario	Commission for Labor Cooperation, Secretariat	
Indiana Villagarcía	University of Texas, Austin	United States
Irene Villalta	Commission for Labor Cooperation, Secretariat	
John Vincent	Commission for Labor Cooperation, Secretariat	
Henry W. Wells	Canadian Consulate General	Canada
Tamara Wisdom	University of Texas, Dallas	United States
Edward Wolff	New York University, New York City	United States
Francisco Zapata	El Colegio de México	Mexico

ABBREVIATIONS AND ACRONYMS

AFL–CIO: American Federation of Labor–Congress of Industrial Organizations

APEC: Asia–Pacific Economic Cooperation

BCNI: Business Council on National Issues (Canada)

BLS: Bureau of Labor Statistics

CAFTA: Canada–United States Free Trade Agreement

CANACINTRA: Cámara Nacional de la Industria de la Transformación (National Chamber of the Manufacturing Industry of Mexico)

CCE: Consejo Coordinador Empresarial (Commission of the Management Coordinator Council, Mexico)

CLC: Canadian Labour Congress

CLSC: local community service center (Canada)

COLMEX: El Colegio de México

CONASAMIN: Comisión Nacional de los Salarios Mínimos (Mexican Minimum Wage Commission)

CONCAMIN: Confederación Nacional de Cámaras Industriales (Mexican Confederation of Industrial Chambers)

COPARMEX: Confederación Patronal de la República Mexicana (Labor Advisor Committee of the Management Confederation of the Republic of Mexico)

CPI: Consumer Price Index

CPI-U: Consumer Price Index for All Urban Consumers

CSN: Conféderation des syndicats nationaux (Confederation of National Trade Unions, Canada)

CTM: Confederación de Trabajadores de México (National Committee of Mexican Confederation of Workers)
ECI: Employment Cost Index
ERC: Employee Relations Committee (United States)
FTA: Free Trade Agreement
GATT: General Agreement on Tariffs and Trade
GDP: Gross Domestic Product
ILO: International Labour Office
IMF: International Monetary Fund
IMSS: Instituto Mexicano del Seguro Social (Mexican Institute for Social Security)
INEGI: Instituto Nacional de Estadística, Geografía e Informática (National Institute of Statistics, Geography, and Informatics, Mexico)
INFONAVIT: Instituto del Fondo Nacional de la Vivienda para los Trabajadores (National Institute for Workers' Housing, Mexico)
ITAM: Instituto Tecnológico Autónomo de México
IUE: International Union of Electrical Workers
LPA: Labor Policy Association (United States)
NAALC: North American Agreement on Labor Cooperation
NAFTA: North American Free Trade Agreement
NAHR: National Academy of Human Resources (United States)
NAIRU: Non-Accelerating Inflation Rate of Unemployment
NAO: National Administrative Office
NBER: National Bureau of Economic Research (United States)
OECD: Organization for Economic Cooperation and Development
OIT: Organización Internacional del Trabajo (International Labour Office)
OPT: Office of Productivity and Technology (United States)
PPP: purchasing power parity
PWT: Penn World Tables
RGDP: real GDP
RGDPCH: real GDP per capita based on a chain index
RGDPEA: real GDP per equivalent adult
RGDPL: real GDP per capita Laspeyres
RGDPW: real GDP per worker

SECOFI: Secretaría de Comercio y Fomento Industrial (Secretariat of Commerce and Industrial Promotion, Mexico)

STARS: Socioeconomic Time-series Access and Retrieval System

STPS: Secretaría del Trabajo y Previsión Social (Secretariat of Labor and Social Welfare, Mexico)

TFP: Total Factor Productivity

UAW: United Auto Workers (United States)

UNAM: Universidad Nacional Autónoma de México

USX: U.S. Steel Corporation

WTO: World Trade Organization